VOICES OF ALOHA
MAGICAL MAUI

Written and Photographed
by Norman G. Bezane

I went to Maui to stay a week and remained five. I never spent so pleasant a month before, or bade any places good-bye so regretfully. I have not once thought of business or care or human toil or trouble or sorrow or weariness, and the memory of it will remain with me always.

- Mark Twain

ENJOY!

VOICES OF ALOHA SERIES
VOICES OF MAUI: NATIVES AND NEWCOMERS
MAUI FOR MILLIONS
VOICES OF ALOHA
VOICES OF ALOHA MAGICAL MAUI

Norm

AVIVA
PUBLISHING
New York

Ordering Information: norm.mauiauthor@gmail.com
Special discounts are available on quantity purchases by corporations, associations, and others.

Published by Aviva, New York, for Voices of Maui Talk Story, LLC, Lahaina, Hawaii

Cover: "Ka'anapali," courtesy Jim Kingwell, Kingwell Island Art
Cover and Book Design: Meredith Lindsay

Second Edition

ISBN: 978-1-943164-77-6

CONTENTS

ONE
POLYNESIANS, KINGS, and QUEENS:
A TREACHEROUS TALE

The Hawaiian pear is now fully ripe and this is the golden hour for the United States to pluck it.
—US Minister John Stevens

TWO
THE VISITOR EXPERIENCE

People save their whole lives to come to Hawaii. What a blessing to have them here.
—Dale Simonsen

THREE
TODAY'S HAWAIIANS and THEIR CULTURE

My goal is to educate people so they know the preciousness of what makes Hawaii and Maui separate from the rest of the world and we have something to offer during these turbulent years.
—Ed Lindsey

FOUR
ENTERTAINERS/ARTISTS

Would you live anywhere else?
—Musician Willie K.

FIVE
MAKERS OF MODERN MAUI

I'm a cliff jumper.
—Visionary Theo Morrison

SIX
REMARKABLE PEOPLE HERE and ABOUT

Aloha is a two-way street. If you are nice, we are nice.
—Octogenarian Blackie Gadarian

AFTERWORD

I do hereby solemnly protest against any and all acts done against myself and the Constitutional Government of the Hawaiian Kingdom.
—Queen Liliʻuokalani

Flower leis and their aroma symbolize one of the many reasons people have a passion for Maui

PASSION FOR MAUI

People's love affair with Maui, once ignited, is never ending and there is never a divorce.
—The Author

FROM CALIFORNIA to New York, from Europe, from Montreal to Mexico, from Australia to Aruba, from Japan and now China, 2.5 million people land on a mid-Pacific island farther from land than most any other. Some keep the dour expressions of back home. Many, however, show that Maui glow. The glow expresses enchantment with the place.

An insurance broker from the Virgin Islands a while back exits Kahului airport, notices the aroma of fragrant plumeria, feels the trade wind breezes, and knows she has to live on the island of Maui. Six months later, she is in a new home. The experience is not uncommon for new arrivals.

Love of Maui brings visitors back again and again and often evokes comments that one day they would like to live here. Some eventually do.

For some, love grows into a passion. There are other Hawaiian Islands. For none is there the kind of passion you can find for Maui.

Travel magazines have named Maui the world's best island. Maui No Ka Oi ("Maui is the best"). Hawaiians said that centuries ago. It is still true.

A journalist and his bride come on honeymoon. Over a few years, they vacation on a Caribbean island where the sun sets in the wrong place. It's not America, and there's no aloha for tourists.

So the husband, this author, says, "Why are we trying to find a place as nice as Maui? Let's go there every year." And we do. Years later, a daughter marries and a new son-in-law wonders: "What is all this fascination with Maui? The new son-in-law comes with new wife on his first trip to Maui. And then he knows. He gets it. A year later, he is talking about his next trip and what he will do. Go to Mama's Fish House, Maui's premier restaurant situated on a lovely cove with white-capped waves crashing ashore from a deep-blue ocean, a brilliant blue sky overhead with fluffy white clouds, and a surging wind that propels colorful sails along the coast.

People's love affair with Maui, once ignited, is never ending and there is never a divorce.

A frequent visitor from Washington State expresses it best on these pages. She tells she her companion: "I want my ashes spread here. If I die here, don't send me back. I am home."

One day, it is likely she will get her wish, as will the author and his bride now of 46 years. (We tell newlyweds that a honeymoon on Maui is a great start. Just look at us.)

For the author, there will be a celebration of life attended by remarkable people of aloha. It will include many pictures—laughing on St Patrick's Day at the Lahaina Yacht Club, walking through a rainforest, coasting on a bike down Haleakala Crater, on a picnic in a grassy field on the way to Hana, introducing a grandson to the Pacific Ocean, enjoying a luau with relatives, attending a community festival, and much more.

Loved ones will board a flower-decked canoe. A conch shell will blow. And the ashes will waft through the tropical breeze and fall into the sea.

QUINTESSENTIAL BEACH WALK

This is one of the few places on earth people have a passion for.
— "Morning Goddess," KPOA

ON THE BEACH WALK at Kaʻanapali Beach Resort, site of the most popular and best beach on Maui, visitors find a summation of the Maui experience. They will use this as a base for a few days of exploring the island.

Visitors will enjoy the sweeping ocean views, waterfalls, and a bamboo forest on the road to Hana. They thrill at a rainbow of colors at dawn over 10,000-foot Haleakala Crater.

Back down the mountain, likely as not, they will visit the historic cowboy town of Makawao or the former sixties hippie haven of Paia and then cross the *pali* (cliffs) to return to historic Lahaina, former capital of the Hawaiian Kingdom, modern-day place for evening experiences.

Another day, visitors will sample the North Shore on a winding onelane road to see the ocean crashing through a blowhole. The twisty road gives way to the rocky shores of Kapalua a few miles from Kaʻanapali Beach again.

For many jet-lagged early risers, though, the love for Maui begins on the beach path at dawn when the sun peaks over the West Maui Mountains. Sometimes a light sprinkling of rain will produce an arching 180 degree rainbow above Kaʻanapali Beach that will frame Lanaʻi and Molokaʻi still slumbering in darkness. Shadows of stately palms begin to appear as silhouettes on the golden beach as the sun rises.

Maui one year was named the world's best island. Twice the same publication proclaimed Kaʻanapali the world's best beach. Small birds twitter. Bright yellow hibiscus, scarlet and yellow bougainvillea, spidery white lilies with scarlet tips line

*The quintessential beach path
steps from the beach is a magnet
for visitors from early morning to
evening and beyond*

the path that is beginning to fill with strollers.

This day, cresting waves white with foam noisily splash to shore. Later, barechested Hawaiians will stand silently with their surfboards placed vertically into the sand. At precise moments, one at a time, they will grab their boards, race to the swells, and once about every six tries manage a perfect somersault as they land in the sea and prepare to return to the next good wave.

Beyond Canoe Beach where canoe clubs gather on a Saturday morning for a morning paddle, the Hyatt (more formally known as the Hyatt Regency Resort and Spa) springs to life. Two majestic white swans glide along against the backdrop of a Japanese garden. Attendants have already covered row upon row of chaise lounges with brilliantly hued yellow towels to await morning sunbathers.

Maui's luminescent sun, favored by artists because of the beautiful light it casts, has a special way of accentuating colors—rich, deep hues that a keen observer sees all along the path. Past a short tree with clusters of yellow-tinged plumeria the scene shifts to the Marriott, its 35 oceanfront lounges on a narrow swath of grass with stark white towels laid out standing there as if they were sentinels up and ready for duty. The early risers, after first sampling the beach, head to the new Starbucks with its killer views better than almost any to be found at a coffee shop back home.

Sipping lattes at outdoor tables where birds fly about searching for crumbs, visitors get their news from a miniature handout version of the New York Times and sometimes rise to view humpback whales in all their magnificence breaching offshore. The first iPhones of the day are whipped out for a futile attempt to photograph the world's largest mammals, here each year from Alaska.

Walking happily along, visitors who wouldn't dream of

saying good morning to a passerby at home offer a greeting or a soft "aloha." A few of the newly arrived wear crimson airport leis. The apparel of choice is a T showcasing the colleges they went to. An old guy who knows he is old shows it with a T-shirt that proclaims, "Old Guys Rule." If he thinks he is old, he is old. He doesn't know old guys don't rule.

Farther along the path, beach boys wearing luminescent orange shirts teach visitors how to stand up on a paddleboard. The newcomers stretch out prone on their boards to learn the techniques on still another carefully manicured Marriott lawn. At sea, on placid ocean days, paddlers already are moving over the gentle swells. Farther down, guests will soon be fishing, taught by instructors in Marriott red. Inviting but empty hammocks sway in the breeze awaiting little girls who will insist on hopping on with mom.

Next, at the Ali'i condominium, attendants clean sleek new stainless-steel barbecue grills, whiffs of sizzling steaks from the evening before long gone. At the Westin, two speckled pale green sculpted frogs beckon little ones. A fierce ancient Chinese warrior in blue-gray stone stands guard clutching a sword in one hand and a single red hibiscus in another placed there by a playful Westin worker. Deep-blue umbrellas above lounges line the beach. The soft sound of a cascading resort waterfall fills the air.

More blue. The boutique shopping center Whalers Village looms up, six light-blue flags imprinted with whales waving in the wind against a deep-blue sky. Louis Vuitton handbags and Rolex watches will be on sale for the prosperous.

At 11:00 a.m., chefs at the popular Hula Grill and Leilani's on the Beach whip up the first fish tacos and mahi-mahi sandwiches. Servers in aloha blouses get ready to dish up Hula Pie, five inches tall, with a chocolate crust and a tower of vanilla ice cream topped with whipped cream. The slice is usually shared by two.

At about 4:30 p.m. this Saturday, a packed crowd of visitors and regulars at Leilani's cheer musician JD playing "Sweet Caroline" as they touch hands. Harry Troupe plays his guitar held behind his back to more cheers.

A crowd lines up on the beach and soon families splash through the surf, climb a narrow ladder, and board a tall-masted catamaran. Four of the twin-hulled vessels will return at sunset to form a kind of catamaran rush hour as the sun departs behind Moloka'i.

Dozens of visitors dressed for dinner flock to the Whalers Village lawn. There's a Nikon or two, but usually an Apple or Samsung phone held for a selfie with the setting sun beyond varying in quality each day. There is little elbowroom.

At the "Most Hawaiian Hotel" near a whale-shaped swimming pool, locals and visitors gather at the Tiki Bar. Dale, who has poured more than 400,000 mai tais during his 40-year career, jokes with customers. A nightly hula show begins, the graceful moves of colorful dancers decked out in long dresses with little girls swaying below to imitate their moves.

Night with its cornucopia of stars is about to arrive at the Sheraton, built alongside Pu'u Keka'a, known as "Black Rock." A muscular Hawaiian with a torch produces a thunderous noise with a conch shell, runs across the beach, climbs the volcanic rock lighting torches along the way, stops at the top, and faces north, south, east, and west.

This is the sacred place where Hawaiians believe souls depart for heaven. A king once dove regularly from the cliff in a show of manliness. Today's diver removes a flower lei from his neck, sends it and the torch cascading into the deep, and dives into the sea.

Aloha is everywhere, from the way visitors are greeted to the word celebrated graphically

LIVING ALOHA

Aloha is not an affectation. It is real.
—The Author

"IN HAWAII, WE GREET FRIENDS, loved ones, and strangers with aloha, which means love," the great Olympic champion Duke Kahanamoku once said.

You have heard it as a luau begins, at music venues, ice cream parlors, and ABC stores sometimes pronounced in three syllables: A…lo…HA. And you hear some simply pronounce it in one breath.

Aloha is not an affectation. It is real. Despite the popular bumper sticker, aloha is not practiced. It is lived and comes from within.

One theory is that the word aloha sprang from the missionaries since compassion for others was at the heart of the Christian message. Aloha has within it the word *ha,* which means breath in Hawaiian.

Even to this day, many Hawaiians greet each other with an exchange of ha. Impressed with this distinctive way of acknowledging others, missionaries may have incorporated the two letters in a word they believed was at the core of what they wanted to preach.

Still others argue that living aloha was a way of life long before the first tall sailing ship landed on these shores.

Aloha is empathy for others that resides in the heart, and it can be acquired naturally if given a chance. Aloha can take the form of a smile, a friendly manner, or an act of kindness. Growing up in Hawaii in cherished *na ʻohana* (family groups), Hawaiians learn aloha ha by example in youth and see it flourish in adulthood. Newcomers can become persons of aloha too and many of them do.

Aloha is an acquired approach to living that is available to those of us who live here, those who are passionate about

Hawaii, and to newcomers and visitors who catch the spirit. Aloha, however, is not automatic. There are some Hawaiians (those with Hawaiian blood) who find the concept of aloha alien.

Duke Kahanameka wrote, "In Hawaii, aloha is the key word to the universal spirit of real hospitality that makes Hawaii renowned as the world's center of understanding and fellowship. Try meeting or greeting people with aloha. You will be surprised by their reaction. I believe it, and it is my creed. Aloha to you."

Pastor Laki Kaʻ is fond of saying there would be no aloha without Hawaii. The good news is you can find aloha without even looking for it. Aloha is just one of many of the island's gifts to the world.

ONE
POLYNESIANS, KINGS, and QUEENS:
A TREACHEROUS TALE

The Hawaiian pear is now fully ripe and this is the golden hour for the United States to pluck it.

—US Minister John Stevens

Queen Lili'uokalani, the last of Hawaiian monarchs.

NEWCOMERS
Once Upon a Time There Was an Island

ONCE UPON A TIME—the year was 1778—a British sea captain named Cook landed on a majestic set of islands. Polynesians had discovered them thousands of years ago.

The people he found were ruled by *ali'i nui* (highest level of leaders). The entire population believed in the philosophy known as pono, or righteousness—doing the right thing by caring for the land and its people and living in perfect harmony with the universe.

The people, as stewards of the land, knew that if they would malama (care for the land) and its *kalo* (taro), the land would care for them and feed them. At a later time, this concept of *pono* was turned into a motto *"ua mau ka ea o ka a'ina i ka pono,"* the life of the land is perpetuated in righteousness. Even now this remains the official motto of the place called Hawaii.

Many moons after Cook died at the hands of natives on the shores of Kealakehua Bay on the island of Hawaii, another sailing ship arrived carrying people known as Calvinists from a place called New England.

Cook, from England, viewed the natives as "a handsome people, hospitable, friendly, and cheerful, living in a beautiful land."

"These were a strong and hardworking people skilled in crafts and possessing much learning," another early observer noted. The Calvinist leader from New England, however, described a different people—a people viewed as naked savages.

The Calvinist missionaries arrived shortly after a great king named Kamehameha died. Death had become—and would continue to be—a frequent visitor.

From the beginning, the men who came in sailing ships

after Captain Cook brought with them diseases. Early records are scarce, but typhoid fever arrived in 1804. Other epidemics followed: influenza in 1826; whooping cough in 1832; mumps in 1839; leprosy in 1840; measles, more whooping cough, and more influenza in 1848; smallpox in 1853; diphtheria in 1890; cholera in 895; and even bubonic plague in 1899–1900.

An estimated million native people dwindled to 200,000 by 1820, 40,000 by 1893, and fewer and fewer in the early twentieth century.

The missionaries brought with them wives and children and settled on coastal lands to preach the good news to the heathen natives. The *Kanaka Maoli* (Native Hawaiians) in many respects were as spiritual in their own way as their new teachers. And thus the Native Hawaiians became willing converts to the new religion.

Missionaries told the natives that the tremendous loss of life resulted from natives worshiping the wrong God. The natives believed the story, and the kings and queens led the way by converting to Christianity.

The missionaries also concluded that the Hawaiians needed a written language. They created an alphabet of 12 letters. The industrious Hawaiian people, seekers of enlightenment, soon became the most literate people in the world as they read newly printed Bibles rendered in the new Hawaiian language.

Almost two decades after the missionaries first arrived, a minister named Hiram Bingham declared that Hawaiians should abandon the concept of pono and make Christianity the cornerstone of their existence. He said old Hawaiian customs had to be abandoned. Christianity and capitalism, including private ownership of the land, would be what was pono.

Some of the sons and daughters of the Calvinist mission-aries developed another passion: King Sugar.

To grow the sugar, they needed to acquire a great deal of land—land used in common by the people and that no one owned. These newcomers, known as businessmen, pressured the king to declare what became known as the "Great Ma-hele." The kingdom's undivided land—4.1 million acres of it—would be divided up.

King Kamehameha III, considered one of the smartest of the monarchs, allotted the kingdom itself 1.5 million acres (36 percent). He allotted one million acres (24 percent) to himself. These became known variously as crown or ceded lands, and sovereignty advocates are still fighting over own-ership of them today.

Just 84,165 acres, less than one percent of the total dis-tributed landmass, were awarded to the common people, and those who acquired plots got a average of three acres each. Also, in appreciation for bringing Christianity and literacy to the islands, each missionary was awarded land—526 acres each.

Some 1.6 million acres, or 39 percent, were converted into private ownership given to 251 *ali'i* (local chiefs), in effect allowing any of them to sell their holdings to anyone they chose. Many of the *ali'i*, who coveted foreign goods, were in debt to foreigners. Foreigners had the money. *Ali'i* had the land.

Through the Great Mahele and the associated Kuleana Act of 1850, foreigners were allowed to acquire land ownership for the first time. So-called *'ohana* lands shared by the people could now be exchanged for money.

And so it came to pass after a number of years that 95 percent off the cherished land came under the control of just 82 major private landowners, including many who built giant companies, some still in operation today. Britain and the United States also had their eyes on the land, considering the islands a strategic place that could be used to protect and provide services for their interests in the Pacific. Lord Paulet in 1843 declared the Hawaiian Islands a possession of Great Britain, starting a legacy still present in the form of a Union Jack on Hawaii's state flag.

Select numbers of Americans wanted more than land. They wanted control of the Hawaiian government. In 1893, they organized, in effect, a coup d'état to take the Hawaiian Kingdom away from Queen Lili'uokalani. In an amazingly speedy turn of events, a Committee of Safety, falsely formed to protect lives and property during a period of supposed unrest, called in the US Marines on January 16, 1893, to restore order.

On January 17, people who wanted to protect their business interests and who were not Hawaiians declared the establishment of a provisional government. Just 11 days later, after a long sea journey, representatives of the new "government" arrived in San Francisco on their way to Washington, DC. And six days later, they made it to the American capital.

Six days after that, a treaty of annexation to bring the islands under the control of the United States was introduced in the US Senate. A representative of the United States to the new "government" in Honolulu named Stevens opined, "The Hawaiian pear is now fully ripe, and this is the golden hour for the United States to pluck it."

In 1898, Hawaii was officially annexed. And in 1900, it became an official US territory. Nearly 60 years after that, Hawaii became a state.

After the land division, great plantation towns eventually grew up in Lahaina, Wailuku, Paia, and elsewhere. They filled up with new immigrants—Chinese, Japanese, Koreans,

Portuguese, and Filipinos—to meet the demand for labor that could not be supplied by diminishing numbers of Hawaiians. Some 65,000 Asians alone arrived around 1890.

Twelve decades after the arrival of the missionaries came a rising power to the east, a foreign power sent waves of war machines swooping in to strike a blow against the United States at a place called Pearl Harbor. Soldiers, sailors, and marines came to help out their comrades. After four years of fighting throughout the Pacific, some stayed and some vowed to one day return.

On Maui, the land was transformed. Green waves of sugarcane covered the mountains. Pineapple fields blossomed with row upon row of succulent fruit grown, harvested, and sent to big canneries that packed and prepared the pineapple for shipment to the mainland.

Finally, powerful winged aircraft called jet airplanes were invented, providing relatively easy access to this paradise in the middle of the Pacific. King Sugar gave way to King Tourism. Luxury hotels, condominiums, and cramped quarters called timeshares arose. Once-in-a-lifetime trips to paradise were turned into annual jaunts. The rich, famous, and newly affluent came. They built million-dollar homes where taro patches once flourished.

New lifestyles appeared, practiced by locals out of touch with Hawaiian roots and newcomers called malihini. Hawaiians—once told to abandon their customs, drop their language, and forget their past—began to recognize how much they had lost. And so began the "Hawaiian Renaissance," a revival of the culture.

In the words of popular fairy tales, it is still unclear whether the people lived happily ever after.

ALI'I LEADERS
Ali'i Rule Through Pain of Death

THERE'S THE KA'ANAPALI ALI'I, Ali'i Dry Cleaners, and even Ali'i Computer Services. Perhaps not such a good idea, since the actions of these Hawaiian chiefs were mixed.

Ali'i ruled their moku (districts) for centuries. King Kamehameha, of course, was the first to rule over all of the Hawaiian Islands. In the 1830s, Lahainaluna was more like a college than a high school. David Malo, 38, was one of its best student-scholars.

The historian is respected so much that a David Malo Day celebration is held every year way up Lahainaluna Road at the school.

Malo wrote that in ancient times Hawaiians in need of government appointed a king whose job was to "gather the people in time of war and decide all important questions of state concerning the life and death of the common people." It was also his duty to consecrate temples and oversee religious rites.

Before the arrival of Tahitians in 800 AD, most everybody on Maui was considered equal. Then, a higher class of people, the *ali'i,* were appointed to keep everything running smoothly, sometimes with deadly force.

A chief of high rank was not allowed to have children with a woman of lesser rank. A suitable partner for a chief of the highest rank to preserve the bloodlines was his sister. Their offspring would be of the highest rank.

Ali'i had six different names for the offspring of different kinds of kingly parents. A man who was given a gift of land by an *ali'i,* for example, was known as an *ali'i kau holo papa,* a chirf of lesser rank.

Death was the penalty for disrespecting an ali'i. Commoners could be put to death if they raised a knee when kneeling before an *aliʻi* (required), launched a canoe at the same time as an aliʻi, or stepped into the shadow of an *aliʻi* during daylight.

If traveling by day, a flag bearer would call out "*kapu moe*," causing commoners to prostrate themselves. When personal possessions, such as a chief's clothing or food, were being carried, anyone who remained standing was put to death.

A king could put to death or spare a commoner with a single word. There was no penalty for murder. Thus, Malo wrote, most commoners lived in fear.

If they survived, Hawaiians were keen observers of land, sea, and even human behavior. They had 33 different names for various conditions in the ocean, 14 names for different kinds of clouds, nine names for winds, four names for various kinds of rain, seven names for the time of day, and 30 names for days of the month.

Though comfortable putting people to death, the ancients had far more than the fabled seven deadly sins. They had as many as 32 words for human frailties, including deceit (*hoʻopunipuni*) and lying (*waha he*).

One word that does not appear in Malo's extensive index is aloha. Its embrace by many of today's Hawaiians and malihini (newcomers) who have taken up residence here must mean that there has been progress. And today, at least according to the Declaration of Independence, all men and women are created equal.

KING KAMEHAMEHA THE GREAT
Warrior, Unifier, Surfer, Trader, Shaper of Maui

POWERFULLY BUILT, SQUARE-JAWED WARRIOR King Kamehameha the Great completed the unification of the Hawaiian Islands. Ten years before, he conquered all of Maui, Lana'i, and Moloka'i. Kamehameha's decisions in the early 1800s shaped Maui as we know it today.

When locals think of Kamehameha, we think of King Kamehameha III Elementary School named after his son, the famous Kamehameha Schools, Kamehameha Avenue in Kahului, and even the official Kamehameha Day state holiday in June. .

Few remember that a nuclear submarine was named for this Hawaiian and that his statue is in a place of honor in the US Capitol at the National Statuary Hall.

Kamehameha did not cut down a cherry tree, nor did he wear wooden false teeth, yet he could be considered the George Washington of these islands.

If alive today, the great king would probably lash out at the comparison, since he was a great fan of Great Britain, a country he considered a protector of the islands.

Kamehameha was born of *ali'i* (kingly) heritage on the island of Hawaii, unified the islands, was a fierce warrior, and had the physique of a tall, muscular NBA player. The fascination is in the detail.

Kamehameha—his name means the one who is set apart—was destined for glory as the son of two high chiefs, including one of Oahu's most powerful warriors, from the day of his birth.

Some believe the future king was born in 1758 at about the time of Halley's Comet and that he was the powerful king mentioned in prophecies.

The fledgling king already had mega *mana* derived from two royal parents that each had considerable mana in their own right. *Mana* was acquired by inheritance or heroics in battle. Battles were often fought to acquire more *mana*.

According to tradition, Kamehameha got more even more *mana* when he acquired the hair of the slain Captain Cook, explorer of much of the Pacific Rim. Hawaiians believed Cook also had a lot of *mana*.

The remains of the man who named these Sandwich Islands were divided up after his death on the beach near Kona. Kamehameha, an admirer of Cook, had visited his ships, even though he had nothing to do with the explorer's demise. Historical facts complete the story.

Trained to be a fierce warrior, Kamehameha fought his first battle on Maui at 17 in an unsuccessful effort by a Hawaiian chief to conquer the island.

Kamehameha returned again and again to Maui's Iao Valley to Lahaina's shoreline, to the rough volcanic landscape of the island of Hawaii, and to the newly discovered harbor in Honolulu he decided was the ideal place to foster trade. Both epic and trivial, these journeys transformed Hawaii.

In 1783, the man who was to become great launched his campaign to unify these islands. Kamehameha had fought his first battle on Maui at 17 in an unsuccessful effort by a Hawaiian ali'i (king) to conquer the island.

Later, after moving a 5,000-pound stone called Naha, which legend said could be moved only by a man of destiny, the powerfully built warrior with the fierce face set forth on his life's work of conquest.

To invade Oahu, in a feat of organization, Kamehameha assembled 36,000 warriors transported in 800 canoes. Kamehameha organized his units in groups of 400. Thus, he marshaled 900 sets of troops (36,000) and two groups of canoes (400 each).

Trained warriors led by ali'i fought to take over land of both living *ali'i* and the recently deceased. warrior. Some 200 years ago, the powerfully built, square-jawed warrior completed the unification of the Hawaiian Islands after conquering Oahu, Maui, Lana'i, and Moloka'i.

His exploits are richly described in dozens of books by numerous illustrious historians—Lahaina's David Malo included. Kamehameha was born of ali'i (kingly) lineage on the island of Hawaii. He had the physique of a tall, muscular NBA player.

Some believe the future monarch was born in 1758 at about the time of Halley's Comet, an event mentioned in prophecies as signaling the birth of a powerful king.

The fledgling king already had mega mana (a word meaning acquired authority, power, and prestige) derived from two royal parents who each had considerable *mana* of their own. Mana was acquired by inheritance or heroics in battle. Battles were often fought to acquire more *mana.*

Tradition says Kamehameha got even more *mana* when he acquired the hair of the slain Captain Cook, explorer of the Pacific Rim. Hawaiians believed Cook also had a lot of mana.

The remains of the man who named these Sandwich Islands were treated in the traditional manner after his death on the beach near Kona. The flesh was deboned and the bones wrapped in *kapa* (tapa) cloth in such a way that no sound could enter. The bones were then hidden.

Kamehameha, an admirer of Cook, had visited his ships, although that had nothing to do with the explorer's demise.

Kamehameha fought his first battle on Maui at 17 in an unsuccessful effort by a Hawaiian ali'i (king) to conquer the island.

Later, after moving a 5,000-pound stone called Naha, which legend said could be moved only by a man of destiny, the powerfully built warrior with the fierce face set forth on his life's work of conquest.

Wars were declared by cutting down a coconut tree in another's territory. Battles were fought according to rituals, traditions, and rules.

Weapons of choice were the elau (short spear), pololu ihe (long spear), palau (cudgel), leiomano (club with sharks' teeth), and later guns. War and weapons would be put aside with the unification of the islands.

A clear picture of what Kamehameha did, and how he did it, emerges by looking at his travels.

1778, Hana: Meets Captain Cook and discovers unique sticks that fire bullets. He has the foresight to see their potential in battle.

1783, Island of Hawaii: Starts campaign to unify islands by unsuccessfully attacking Hilo.

1785, Hilo: Hawaii A new attack.

1788, Kauai: Trades land he controls for guns, including a swivel cannon. Captures sailor John Young, kidnaps Isaac Davis, and then names them military advisors.

1790, Maui: Fights near Huelo and uses cannon for the first time in the Iao Valley. Blood and bodies clog the stream, giving the fight the name "Kepaniwai" (Damming of the Water). Leaves before conquering Maui.

1791, Island of Hawaii: Builds Pu'ukohola *Heiau* temple to win support of the gods for his unification effort. Uses swivel gun and cannon to win the battle and conquer the island.

1792–94, Period of peace.

1793, Befriends Captain George Vancouver, who was also acquainted with beautiful, Hana-born Ka'ahumanu, a surfing partner who became the king's first and favorite wife. Vancouver gives Kamehameha cattle, sheep, and goats. Ka'ahumanu along the way deserted Kamehameha, after he flirted with Ka'ahumanu's sister. Vancouver is instrumental in bringing the two back together.

1794, Announces that Hawaiian people are subjects of Great Britain and under its protection. Great Britain never agreed, but Vancouver gifts Kamehameha with a sailing ship with a Union Jack sail.

1795,Maui and Oahu: Destroys Lahaina and then conquers Maui, Lana'i, and Moloka'i in February. Sails to Oahu and wins Battle of Nu'uunu on the windward side of Waikiki to control Oahu. Leader of Kauai eludes capture.

1796, Kauai: Invades Kauai for the second time.

1797, Takes a second wife in Keopuolani, who bears him a son, Liholiho, who succeeds Kamehameha as king. Ka'ahumanu, though childless, would later rule as regent for the young Liholiho and become Hawaii's first "feminist," ending the *kapu* (forbidden) system that banned *kane* and *wahine* (men and women) from eating together.

1802, Maui: Fleet lands in Maui to prepare to invade Kauai again. A storm overwhelms warriors and ends expedition.

1803: Honolulu: Sends fleet to new harbor and headquarters there. Kamehameha believes the Oahu harbor is better for loading ships (Lahaina harbor was too shallow to permit docking of sailing ships). Becomes a trader, taking over the lucrative sandalwood trade and sending wood to China in exchange for worldly goods.

1810, Completes unification by acquiring Kauai by agreement with the ali'i Kaumuali'i without a fight.

1812–19, Kohala, Island of Hawaii: Returns to birth island. Engages in his favorite pastimes of surfing, swimming, fishing, and growing taro. Dies in 1819.

2016, Front Street, Lahaina: Kamehameha images grace annual parade. Each Kamehameha Day, horseback riders on the former King's Highway pass within yards of where Kamehameha the Great once surfed, lived, and enjoyed the King's Taro Patch. Kamehameha, in a sense, was a man before his time. He recognized immediately the merits of western technology (guns, for example, which he rarely used).

He lived in three geographic areas like modern-day corporate types, learned a foreign language (English), and created what would become one of the world's most progressive monarchies. Add everything up, and no wonder he is called great.

King Kamehameha the Great, unifier of the islands.

MISSIONARY
Edward Bailey
More Than Meets the Eye

FEWER THAN 50 YEARS after Captain Cook chanced upon the Hawaiian Islands in 1778, the next wave of newcomers came to the land: missionaries.

What most visitors and locals know about missionaries can be concisely summed up in a few short sentences. They came to Wailuku and Lahaina, converted thousands of Hawaiians, designed a Hawaiian alphabet, clashed with sailors, opened schools, and later, some commonly say, grabbed land.

Lahaina's Dwight Baldwin wore two hats as a minister and doctor. Another, Edward Bailey, wore many more. Among newcomers arriving after Cook, Bailey was perhaps Maui's first true Renaissance man.

Bailey's life, starting in Lahaina, is chronicled in a magnificently written and illustrated book by a former president of the Maui Historical Society. It brings to life the missionary experience as few others have.

In Edward Bailey of Maui, Linda McCullough Decker brings to life clearly and insightfully a missionary who has rarely been documented, even though he unselfishly served islanders for more than 40 years.

Missionaries, according to quotations from diaries and other documents Decker researched beginning in 1991, were here to complete the work of saving souls "in the shortest possible time within a single generation."

With his wife, Carolyn—described as a sweet woman by frequently quoted missionary Julia Cooke—Bailey landed in Lahaina to help run Lahainaluna Seminary. Not long after, the couple was transferred to Wailuku to head the Wailuku Female Seminary in 1837.

The school was the counterpart to the boy's institution at Lahainaluna, serving some 50 girls ages up to 12 to turn out versatile Christian women, because Lahainaluna boys would grow up to need marriage partners who would hold the same newly taught values.

Moving into a vacuum when Queen Ka'ahumanu and others renounced the old religion a few years before their arrival, Hawaii's missionaries succeeded like no others, according to Decker. Unlike their counterparts in Ceylon, India, and other places, they were able to convert the chiefs and the reigning *ali'i*.

Hawaiians had reverence not only for their fellow man but for animals, sea creatures of all kinds, the land, and even such objects as trees and lava. The missionaries focused on the salvation of people and "introduced a new lifestyle sustained by trade."

Carolyn asked the missionary board to import all the supplies to sustain the family: "jackets, pantaloons, vests, suspenders, nine yards of gingham, sewing cotton, scissors, ribbons, kettles, pots, plates and tumblers, spices, and 31 gallons of lamp oil."

Seminary girls learned the traditional lessons in Hawaiian and were also taught to sew, spin, and crochet. They also would work an hour a day in their own garden plots.

After only 12 years, the board cut off funding to all of its Maui missionaries, forcing the school to close in 1849.

A common belief to this day is that first- and second-generation missionaries went after land because of greed. Instead, they turned to farming as a way to support their schools and churches and to make a living.

At least 40 out of 400 missionaries who stayed started businesses that became giant companies, some of which still dominate today.

Decker pointed out that with whaling in decline, missionaries also felt that agriculture was the best way for Hawaiians to sustain themselves—which, incidentally, they had been able to do for thousands of years.

To pursue his real passion to teach, Bailey opened up a second private school. Tuition was $18 a month. That didn't last long either.

The versatile Bailey went on to make a living every way he could, surveying lands for pay. As a surveyor, he laid the routes for roads from Lahaina over the Pali to Makawao. He drew boundaries near Wailuku and bought land in Kula that later became part of Haleakala Ranch.

Over the years, he would supervise a school in Kula, serve as Maui health commissioner, and become an agent for a flour company. He started a sugar plantation and turned it over to his son.

He built the first bridge over the Wailuku River, vaccinated for smallpox, taught Sunday school, and helped build Ka'ahumanu Church on High Street.

He also painted majestic watercolors of missionary times and nature that now illustrate the book. He wrote what was described as good poetry, and he was a musician.

In the end, Bailey died penniless and was supported by one of his sons. When someone Upcountry needed a surveyor, he asked "for an honest man like Bailey." And that Bailey was.

QUEEN KA'AHUMANU
First Hawaiian Feminist

SHE WAS CONSIDERED BEAUTIFUL and sprightly. She loved to paddle in canoes, swim, surf, and fly kites. She loved board games, especially checkers, and once beat 20 men on a ship. She once lived steps from the ocean in Lahaina and preferred white dresses like those worn by foreigners.

The favorite of King Kamehameha's 21 wives was born the same year Captain Cook arrived and transformed a kingdom just a few years after its unification by her great husband. Her gradual embrace of newly arrived missionaries paved the way for the new religion and literacy and ended *kapu,* changing the relationship between Hawaiian men and women.

This fascinating lady whose name means "bird of feathers" easily could be regarded as the first Hawaiian feminist (defined for those who did not grow up in the sixties as the belief that men and women should have equal rights and opportunities).

It was Ka'ahumanu who freed women, declaring the end of a practice under which women were forbidden to eat with men or live in the same dwelling with them. Some say Queen Kiopuolani was also respnsible for he demise of the kapu, which involved many customs beyond food.

Ka'ahumanu's greatest impact, however, was on religion and education. She embraced the new Christianity and insisted that all of her subjects learn to read the Bible—an action that helped make Hawaiians the most literate people in the world in the nineteenth century. Showing her prowess, Ka'ahumanu learned to read in three days.

From this and other sources, we learn how Ka'ahumanu lived and reigned as a regent for King Kamehameha II and for the missionaries, becoming their greatest advocate.

Ka'ahumanu was Maui's own. Born in a cave in Hana, she almost drowned as an infant when, swaddled in *tapa* cloth, she fell out of a canoe. Her parents predicted that she would one day become queen.

Her first claim to fame began when she became the favorite wife of King Kamehameha, who would eventually have 20 more wives. A woman became a man's wife if she slept with him just once overnight.)

Ka'ahumanu's life with Kamehameha was a mixed blessing. Flirtatious Ka'ahumanu was not above taking lovers, and the king assigned a small boy to keep an eye on her so she wouldn't stray. She did, and the king had her lover strangled to death.

Luckily for Kamehameha, he had a friend who became a kind of a marriage counselor: renowned English navigator Captain George Vancouver. When the king and queen separated, Vancouver brought them back together. The reconciliation didn't last. After 11 years together, Kamehameha later abandoned Ka'ahumanu for his other wives.

The queen was so distraught that she contemplated suicide by drowning. The story goes that a small boy appeared who also was on the verge of drowning. Ka'ahumanu saved him, and in the process saved herself, setting the stage for more great achievements.

KA'AHUMANU REVISITED
We Can Eat Meat with Men, Queen Declares

NEAR THE KING'S WAY (now Front Street in Lahaina) on the *makai* (ocean) side, the first western-style dwelling in the islands went up in Lahaina in 1798. Kamehameha the Great, who had come to Lahaina with 800 war canoes as part of a strategy to unite the Hawaiian Islands, built the "brick palace" for his favorite wife, the great Queen Ka'ahumanu. Since she was not into western ways at the time, she preferred to stay in a nearby grass hut, according to a plaque placed nearby by the Lahaina Restoration Foundation (LRF).

Spending almost all of her adult life with missionaries, Ka'ahumanu was receptive to their teachings from the beginning, according to author Susanna Moore. She eventually fully embraced the new religion brought by Christians from New England and even began to adopt some western ways.

Ka'ahumanu followed her husband from place to place, living in a compound in Waikiki near the present-day Royal Hawaiian Hotel amid hundreds of grass huts, staying in another grass hut in Lahaina, and then in the ancestral home of Kamehameha on the island of Hawaii.

Ka'ahumanu's first great act occurred when she became regent in 1819, presiding over the kingdom because Kamehameha's successor, his son Liholiho, was too young.

Shortly after she became regent, she ended the *kapu* that prohibited women from eating with men and other forbidden activities that made them second-class citizens. Later, Liholiho—like other monarchs—traveled to England where he succumbed to measles and returned to Hawaii in a burial shroud. Ka'ahumanu extended her positive influence further.

Becoming a believer after spending so much time with missionaries, she became convinced Hawaiians needed to learn to read so they could learn about the new deity in the Bible. At various times, she ordered the printing of 1,000 primers and 3,000 copies of the Sermon on the Mount.

She also sought more books and more schools for her people, and Ka'ahumanu once asked Captain Vancouver to bring back religious instructors from England.

In 1819, Kamehameha the Great died. Despite the fact that the king was known to have beaten her on occasion, Ka'ahumanu mourned in a traditional way by getting tattoos of bird talons and the king's name on her arms and feet.

Coming to understand Christian values, Ka'ahumanu outlawed murder, theft, adultery, prostitution, and fighting, and she banned levying taxes on the poor. She also wanted Hawaiians to observe the Sabbath.

The queen, however, also struck a blow against part of the culture worth preserving. Ka'ahumanu banned hula because she thought it was too sexually suggestive. An important part of Hawaiian life, hula was not revived until the ascension 50 years later in 1874 of King Kalakaua (otherwise known as the Merrie Monarch).

Ka'ahumanu's lifestyle also changed over the years. From a sea captain's stash, she learned to love brandy. Missionaries were not above imbibing either.

Untroubled sitting around naked while talking with missionaries, Ka'ahumanu eventually became enamored with western clothes, including silks, satin gowns, and shawls. In *Paradise of the Pacific*, author Susanna Moore reported that Ka'ahumanu came to want to live like a *haole* (foreigner) and learn domestic arts.

In December 1825, Queen Ka'ahumanu began to contemplate the end of her life and finally agreed to have Hiram Bingham, head of the mission, baptize her. "I am making myself strong," she is quoted as saying. "I do not know when the Lord will come and take me."

Ka'ahumanu would live another seven years and passed away just before sunrise on June 30, 1832, at the age of 54.

LYDIA LILI'UOKALANI
The Last Queen Fights for a Kingdom

OF ALL THE KINGS AND QUEENS in history, perhaps none loved America as much as Her Majesty Lydia Lili'uokalani of the Kingdom of Hawaii. She said so in her writings. In the ultimate irony, it was America that had the tragic final say on her destiny.

A forceful advocate for her people who would eventually travel all the way to Washington, DC, to get her kingdom restored, Lili'uokalani interestingly wasn't shy talking about the motivations of those who betrayed her.

The queen wrote bluntly, "For many years, sovereigns welcomed the advice of Americans who had…settled throughout the islands.

"As they became wealthy and acquired title to lands through the simplicity of our people and their ignorance of values and of the new land laws…their greed…love of power…and schemes (avoided their obligations to us).

"The mercantile element, as embodied in Chamber of Commerce, the sugar planters, and the proprietors of missionary stores, formed a distinct political party.

"Although settled upon us and drawing their wealth from our resources, they were alien to us in their customs and ideas respecting government and desired above all else the extension of their power and to carry out their own special plans of advancement."

Lili'uokalani, upon returning from Europe in 1888, found conspiracy alive in the land. She fought for more than 10 years to resist and then tried to overturn the coup d'état that removed her from leading her people.

1887: A missionary party drafts the so-called Bayonet Constitution, taking power from then-King Kalakaua. The king signs it, fearing assassination if he fails to do so.

1888: King Kalakaua, Lydia's brother, known as the "Merrie Monarch," dies.

January 1891: Lili'uokalani becomes queen, beginning years of internal strife.

1893: US Minister John Stevens conspires to overthrow

the kingdom and supports a provisional government. Li-li'uokalani proposes to rewrite the Bayonet Constitution.
January 14, 1893: Committee of Safety formed by businessmen deposes the queen. She yields authority to avoid bloodshed.

January 16, 1893: US Marines land "to restore order."

1893: James Blount, appointed by the president, conducts an investigation and declares Lili'uokalani "the constitutiona ruler of Hawaii."

February 17, 1893: Conspirators declare the queen guilty of treason for wishing to rewrite the Constitution and other actions, fine her $5,000, and sentence her to imprisonment and five years of hard labor.

September 1893: New government pardons the queen. President Cleveland declares overthrow was "an act of war and wholly without justice."

February 1894: US flag is raised, and a protectorate proclaimed.

July 1894: Provisional government formed; declares Hawaii a republic.

January 1895: Royalists revolt to restore monarchy but are captured.

January 25, 1895: Queen abdicates; receiving warrant for her arrest, she is imprisoned in Iolani Palace for eight months under guard. Forty supporters are jailed.

February 1895: Queen says she will be shot for treason unless she renounces the crown.
February 1895: Military commission tries queen and

then imposes a $5,000 fine and imprisonment with hard labor for five years.

June 1897: Queen asks US president to defeat annexation treaty. Some 17,000 Hawaiians and other residents petition Congress to restore the monarchy.

September 1897: Governor Sanford Dole pardons queen.

July 1898: President McKinley signs annexation treaty.

April 1900: President McKinley names Hawaii a US territory. After spending 19 years in exile in her home at Washington Place across from Iolani Palace, Her Majesty Lydia Lili'uokalani died November 11, 1917.

LILI'UOKALANI REVISITED
America Turns its Back on the Queen

HER MAJESTY Lydia Lili'uokalani was more than the deposed leader of the Hawaiian Islands. She was a world traveler unusual among monarchs, composer of songs still sung today, and a brilliant writer whose autobiography Hawaii's Story by Hawaii's Queen depicts a lady unequalled in her day.

"Immediately after my birth (in 1838)," she wrote, "I was wrapped in the finest *tapa* cloth and taken to the home of another chief by whom I was adopted. At the age of four, I was sent to what was known as the royal school, because its pupils were exclusively persons whose claims to the throne were acknowledged.

"I was a studious girl, and the acquisition of knowledge had been a passion with me during my whole life. The Hawaiian people, from time immemorial, have been lovers of poetry and music and have been apt in improvising historic poems, songs of love, and chants of worship.

"In the early years of the reign of Kamehameha IV, the king brought to my attention that the Hawaiian people had no national aire (anthem). Each nation but ours had its expression of patriotism and love of country. We were using for that purpose, on state occasions, the time-honored British anthem 'God Save the Queen.' In one week's time, I reported to the king I had completed my task (the Hawaiian National Anthem)."

On February 12, 1874, Liliuokalani's brother, King Kalakaua, ascended to the throne. Her younger brother, William Pitt Lili'uokalani, was named his successor, but "the amiable prince was not to live to ascend."

"At noon on the 10th day of April, the booming of the cannon was heard, which announced that I was heir apparent to the throne of Hawaii.

"In the early part of 1878, I was not in enjoyment of my usual good health, and my physician, Dr. Tisdale of Oakland, California, advised a trip to the coast. I obtained my first view of the shores of the great country, the United States, of which land I had heard almost without cession from earliest childhood.

"If first impressions be accepted as auspicious, surely I found nothing of which I could complain on this first visit. Many great citizens of the great city of the Pacific coast came to do us honor."

In 1887, the future queen took another trip to the mainland to tour by train with Queen Kapiolani, taking passage to San Francisco.

"While in San Francisco, the queen improved from an illness to see what she could of the city, this being her first visit to any foreign country.

"In the Rocky Mountains, we passed through great snow sheds (to protect the railroad tracks). The train stopped for a few minutes while our party got off to examine the snow. Taking it up and rolling it into their hands, they made snowballs and pelted each other with them.

"We descended gradually until we reached the Great Salt Lake (Salt Lake City). We stopped for a few hours meeting prominent members of the Mormon Church. The next vivid place I have a recollection of is Denver, which was an infant city. We made no stop in Chicago, and the oil regions of Pennsylvania were the next natural wonders to interest us.

"We arrived safely in Washington, DC. A few days after our arrival, the queen signified our wish to see President Cleveland, and his beautiful young bride most cordially received us."

Next came a trip to Mount Vernon, George Washington's ancestral home. "The rooms that had been used by General Washington, General Lafayette, and Martha Washington were opened to us. The next stop was the tomb, where lie the mortal remains of that great man who assisted at the birth of the nation, which has grown to be so great.

"It seemed to me we were one in our veneration of the sacred spot and the first president of his country. We next visited the city of Boston, and many pleasant excursions were arranged for our party. There was a visit to the Waltham Watch Factory, in which we were very interested.

"In New York, we remained seven days before sailing for England. The queen (Kapiolani) was much interested in her visit to the Metropolitan Museum, the mummies exciting her curiosity and wonder."

Ultimately, the queen and future queen sailed across the Atlantic and reached London to attend the jubilee (fiftieth anniversary) of the ascension of Queen Victoria to the British throne. Many other royal families of the distant world were there, including Prince Komatzu of Japan, the Siamese prince, the brother of the king of Siam, the prince of India, and the prince of Persia.

"Immediately after arrival, Queen Kapiolani sent messages of congratulations to the Queen of Great Britain and Empress of India. The queen received her good wishes with a spirit of cordiality, and thanked her for coming so far to see her." These were the happy days for the future Queen Lili'uokalani, but back home in Hawaii, trouble was brewing.

Capturing a rainbow. A part of visitor experience.

TWO
THE VISITOR EXPERIENCE

People come here from all over the world.

—Music Awards Winner, Henry Kapono

ULTIMATE VISITORS
Chris Marcotte, Gary Bodine
Her Ashes Will Be Here Forever

THEY HANG OUT at the Tiki Bar, often after a summer of sailing around the San Juan Islands in the Northwest. Meet them and the realization comes quickly that they perfectly represent the passion so many have for Maui.

Gary Bodine, a rental specialist who rents his 15 Maui timeshare weeks, and Chris Marcotte, a former massage therapist, frequently listen to some 300 Hawaiian songs Gary has on his iPod on their boat back home in Washington State.

The couple, dividing their time between Maui and Buckley, Washington, regularly cruising the San Juan Islands. Other boaters think they are nuts playing Iz and Grammy winner George Kahumoku on their boat, but they just smile and pretend they are back on Maui. In their own words, this is their story:

Chris: "My passion is Maui. I pack two to three weeks before we come and toss and turn at night since I can't wait."

Gary: "My daughter was very passionate about getting me here and I thought, you know, maybe there is a reason we really need to come. I didn't have a clue what to expect. We stayed at the Royal Lahaina. It was so beautiful.

"We are avid boaters and fishermen and always have been. We have always loved the ocean. My mom, who is 88, said the family has salt in its veins.

"The first day my head was spinning, but I woke up the next morning and we walked along the grounds and along the beach. All of a sudden, it hit me. When someone said it was a tropical paradise, I knew exactly what they meant."

Chris: "The first night there was a full moon, and we had an oceanfront [room]. I stayed up all night watching the moon come up over the water. It was absolutely beautiful."

"We loved it so much the first time we came I wanted to cry when we left. We came for nine days and extended for three more. Normally, we come for a minimum of three weeks and then we extend for a week and then another week.

"And the kids say, 'Are you ever coming home?' And we say, 'Only if we have to.'"

Gary: "We have been coming here for 12 years. It isn't for the pools, and it isn't for activities. We take ourselves on trips around the island to Hana, to Haleakala, and learn as much as we can. After a day or so, we literally drift into tropical paralysis—we are so glad to be here.

"When we went to the Big Island, there was a woman who taught Hawaiian language. She had Hawaiian letters on a Scrabble board. You had to make a Hawaiian word you knew.

"When you are listening to a song, you don't

know what they are singing about. Today, we can look at a street name and know what it means and how to pronounce it. We still don't know much of the language, but what we did learn was that if you look at a word, you know how to pronounce it."

Chris: "Our favorite things are snorkeling at Black Rock (Pu'u Keka'a, where royalty once dove to prove their valor), Honolua Bay, the 14-mile marker, and at Napili (a resort built by Canadians). We go to the hula shows. I don't care how many times I've seen them."

"(At home,) I will go on the computer and look at the Napili Kai and Sheraton webcams every day. (That way) I come here every day."

Chris isn't here full-time yet, because she also loves the San Juan Islands in the summer. But someday, she will be. She movingly sums up her passion this way: "I could live here without a doubt. My heart is here. I want my ashes to be spread here—this is where my soul is."

HONEYMOONERS
Doreen and Damon Stoner
Loving Each Other and Ka'anapali

LOOKING AT THE STRIKINGLY beautiful woman and her handsome husband and seeing them frequently holding hands at a music venue or even during an interview, you would think they were on their honeymoon. Yet they have been married 20 years. Clearly, they are in love with each other and with Kaʻanapali.

Most couples pick a honeymoon location without much thought. Doreen and Damon Stoner, now of Nashville, Tennessee, researched it, talking with travelers on airplanes and consulting guidebooks and magazines (no Internet at the time).

Doreen: "Hawaii seemed like a tropical paradise. It looked like a beautiful place."

Damon: "We wanted someplace special, a peaceful place we were going to remember the rest of our lives."

Today you can run into the Stoners to strike up a conversation most every Fourth of July though they have decided recently to come back during whale season too.

It turns out the Stoners have come to the Hyatt 15 straight years after a first honeymoon trip in 1996. Their Kaʻanapali experiences say a lot about what Kaʻanapali Beach Resort is all about.

"We like the fact everything is nearby. We have made friends—people who appreciate and know us and welcome us back—the staff and even Californians who hop over from LA. When you see so many friends here it just feels like home," Doreen observed.

Damon admits during the year he works constantly. "But I always picture in my mind the waves coming in (on Kaʻanapali Beach). When I am here, I can just relax and decide on my own what we are going to do each day.

"I like to be able to walk up to places, to good restaurants. The Kaʻanapali Beach walk is addictive, and we do it a couple times a day.

"We will eat breakfast, walk down to Black Rock, watch the surf, and people watch." Adds Doreen: "And it is exercise."

The routine, though, is pretty much the same every year. "We have done the touristy things so we mostly relax near the pool. At night, it's Pacific'O, Cheeseburger in Paradise, Lahaina Grill, Cool Cat Café, and, three to four times a trip, Hula Grill down the beach path."

Chicago-reared Damon joined a major pharmaceutical company as a sales rep 23 years ago after securing degrees in chemistry and biology from Indiana University and the University of Illinois. Assignments followed in Chicago, Philadelphia, and Champaign, Illinois.

In Memphis, he met Doreen one night and he found her at another place the next night, promptly inviting her to a James Taylor concert. The romance has been going ever since. It was love at first sight, the two agree.

Doreen worked in sales, recognizing with her husband being transferred so much it would be easy for her to get a job anywhere because salespeople are always in demand. Later she got a master's degree in counseling.

The Stoners are always touting Maui. They tell friends you can spend 10 hours on an airplane to get to a beach or 10 hours in a car to get to someplace not as nice.

Both are clearly good at what they do. Damon volunteers that he has had diabetes for years and heads a support organization when he doesn't have a hectic schedule.

Like many people who love Ka'anapali, they think about living here permanently someday. For now, it is just going to be 10 days around the Fourth of July.

The one disappointment is that performers in training with the awesome Citrus College Band (also a personal favorite) that played afternoon and night for years at the Hyatt no longer come.

Guess the Stoners will just have to confine themselves to going to the pool, strolling the beach path, dining at Hula Grill, and listening to music at Leilani's on the Beach.

MR. ALOHA
Rudy Aquino
Star Showman Brightens Ka'anapali Nights

JUST A FEW HUNDRED YARDS beyond the beach at Ka'anapali, sits one of West Maui's most joyful places—the stage at the Ka'anapali Beach Hotel (KBH).

Strumming his ukulele, pounding on a vibraphone, joking with "the folks," master musician Rudy Aquino has been transforming the center courtyard into a magical oasis of aloha six or seven nights a week for a remarkable eight years.

The masterful showman entertained from 6:00 p.m. to 9:00 p.m. for diners, drinkers, or anyone who wants to sit and watch, free of charge. All comers are welcome.

Guests and regulars appear night after night, or return year after year, to partake of Rudy's musical talents and gift for gab that first gained prominence with the legendary Don Ho.

One never tires of stopping by to hear his incomparable vibes and uke playing, and the lively banter that varies little from night to night never fails to captivate.

The most intriguing thing about Rudy is his enthusiasm, which is on display almost daily alongside his various partners, including Smiley Yoshida, Buddy Jantoc, Ernie Paiva, Ron Hetteen, and others.

Born on the Big Island, Rudy took up piano at 10 when his little sister quit $8 worth of piano lessons on the tenth session. Rudy stepped in at his family's insistence to take the last six lessons. He was hooked.

After his first paid performance at 15, he played honky-tonk piano, the vibes, and percussion instruments at jazz clubs in Old Waikiki and later the Hilton Hawaiian Village. "I was underage in those days, so I had to stand in the sand at the Garden Bar and jump over the wall to join in," he explained. Rudy is quick to report that "when our group, the Ali'is, started with Don Ho, we got equal billing. I will say that again. We had equal billing."

Draft age during the Vietnam War and not interested in toting a gun, Rudy at 22 took his little group and auditioned—as amazing as it might seem—for the US Air Force Band. The air force liked what it heard.

They said yes, so Rudy enlisted, took eight weeks of basic training in Texas, and was shipped to Washington, DC, to play gigs along the East Coast. The highlights included playing for President Kennedy and Jackie at the White House and for the Mercury astronauts.

Rudy performed on Johnny Carson's Tonight Show, in Las Vegas, and in California. Burned out after playing for Don Ho in the seventies and eighties, Rudy settled in Maui in 1988, built two houses, and worked for True Value Hardware in Kula. Missing music, he returned to the stage, ending up at the KBH in 1998.

The Rudy show roars to life with a hula show—usually performed by his wife, Kanoelani; her daughter, Maile Lani; and Ula Nahooikaika.

Following a short break, Rudy may impersonate Elvis, add papaya lyrics to a Neil Diamond song, play the Hawaiian wedding song ("Honeymooners, come on up"), play classic Hawaiian songs, famously render "Phantom of the Opera" on vibes, and even provide cha-cha, waltzes, rumbas, and more for dancing under the stars.

In light of the Iraq War, where his son once served, each performance ends with a rendition of "God Bless America." Visitors from around the world often return to the dance floor to sing and hold hands. Said one twenty-something honeymooner from upstate New York, "Rudy is phenomenal. He appeals to young and old."

For Rudy's spirit and his tales of Hawaiian culture, one is tempted to call him "Mr. Aloha." Yet the real core of Rudy is that he is Mr. Enthusiasm. Leaning on the Tiki Bar with coffee one recent morning, he said, "I don't know why I could do it so long for seven nights a week.

"Something happens on stage; it pushes me. I step on the stage and see people's smiling faces." The smiles are put there by Rudy.

The show ends with cries of "hana hou." (Rudy earlier in the show has taught his new fans that it means "do an encore.")

At 65, Mr. Enthusiasm has no plans to stop playing but nevertheless ended his gig at the hotel to retire to the Cook Islands, much to the chagrin of his many fans.

AQUINO REVISITED
Rudy Aquino
Vibraphonist/Dancer Says "Good Night, Folks"

"HEY FOLKS, we are going to take a short, short break here and come back with our beautiful hula dancers with a nice Hawaiian hula show for you folks. Mahalo and aloha. What a crowd!"

For 15 years—in one stretch seven nights a week for 52 weeks—entertainer, vibraphonist, uke player, and joyful and enthusiastic dispenser of funny lines, Rudy Aquino has been wowing visitors and locals alike at the Tiki Terrace at the KBH.

Joining him in a farewell performance next week will be his favorite beautiful hula dancer, Kanoelani, Rudy's wife of four years. She's completing 15 years on the Tiki stage, including 12 straight years performing nightly.

To the considerable sorrow of his faithful followers—some returning year after year to stay at the place where Rudy plays and Kanoelani dances—the Aquinos will be moving off to "semiretirement" to their beloved Cook Islands, a three-hour flight from Tahiti.

Happening on the pair being interviewed for this column, Robin Kart of the San Francisco Bay area told the couple: "We could stay at the Four Seasons or anywhere, but we have stayed here for 11 years because of your warmth. You've made us feel like family. And you are so genuine.

"You are not doing this because you get paid. The warmth we see comes from within, from your heart."

Though Kanoelani usually speaks with her hips and hula hands, here she talks story, with an occasional pidgin sound mixed in. Born and raised in Japan and China, a navy brat whose father was a pilot, Kanoelani always knew she would wind up in Hawaii, site of many childhood visits.

Kanoelani earlier on was fascinated with Polynesian culture and wanted to learn as much as she could. At 21, she spent six months in Samoa picking coconuts on a plantation before moving to Maui in 1970. Legendary kumu hula (hula teacher) Emma Sharpe, once the sole performer of hula at the growing lineup of hotels in Ka'anapali, taught Kanoelani for five years.

The songs and hulas performed by Emma remain alive to this day, becoming the model for the nightly shows of

Kanoelani and her KBH colleagues who also dance.

Kanoelani lived right next to Sharpe in Kahana and had the task of watering her large lawn—hard work in those days before automatic sprinklers. Kanoelani got respite from this daily chore only when it rained.

With rain clouds coming, Kanoelani would shout for joy. Thus, Emma gave the Caucasian girl who dances with the grace of a Hawaiian the name Kanoelani, which means "mists from heaven."

Kanoelani danced at Cooks on the Beach at the Westin and the old Kapalua Bay Hotel, where she met future husband Rudy Aquino, then playing cocktail-lounge-style piano at the hotel bar.

Together, in 1992, they began their 15-year gig at KBH with Kanoelani in later years sometimes dancing alongside her daughter from her first marriage.

Just before Christmas, Rudy's 'ohana were on hand to see another classic Rudy show that included his signature "Twelve Days of Christmas" with papayas and myna birds substituted for laying hens and turtle doves. The song—sung hilariously with the help of 12 keiki (children), each with a part—was Classic Rudy at his entertainer best.

And that is what Rudy considers himself—an entertainer. In just a few sentences, he explains the philosophy that he tries to teach others. He says there are two types of performers—musicians and entertainers. "If you are a musician, old-school thinking says you belong in a chair with notes in front of you and a conductor. You cannot just take an instrument and play for yourself. You have an obligation," he explained.

"Some people save their whole lives to come here. What a blessing to have them here. So you have an obligation to entertain them, make them happy and comfortable.

You go on stage and there are real people out there.

"You don't stand back; you step right out three feet in front to engage them. You joke with them; you recognize where they are from. You have fun. And you are an entertainer." It is a sad task writing a final tribute. Perhaps the best end is to quote just a few words from classic Rudy:

"Hana hou. Hana hou means to do it again, folks. We are going to do this song for you with a fast beat. This is called 'I Am Hawaii.' Thank you so much, folks, for joining us here this evening. How about a nice hand to Kanoelani for dancing for all of you?

"Before we go, first, we have been having a lot of fun tonight, but we cannot help but recognize all our troops who have been working hard for us. We end every night with this song all about freedom. So, folks, sing along with us: 'God bless America, land that I love.' Good night, folks, and aloha."

CONCIERGE
Malihini Keahi Heath
Bringing the Spirit of Aloha Alive

NAMED MALIHINI—Hawaiian for "newcomer to the land"—she has an apt name. Concierge extraordinaire at what is properly billed as the most Hawaiian hotel, Malihini Keahi-Heath makes the spirit of aloha come alive to other na malihini: first-time, longtime visitors.

Malihini is descended from a Tahitian who came to the islands in 1708. Her eight brothers and sisters have led a far different life than their parents.

Malihini's dad, a fisherman known as Uncle Moon, worked for many years for Pioneer Mill, planting and harvesting cane starting at 6:00 a.m., running heavy equipment, and eventually moving up to supervisor. Off at 2:30 p.m., he'd take a break, have an early dinner, and be off to the Napili Kai Beach Resort to perform as a musician until 10:00 p.m. on many nights.

Mom, known as Auntie Primrose, had a florist shop in Lahaina and used to buy turtles and filet them in her backyard. Three of her eight siblings, including a musician, are involved in the visitor industry. Her five children include a hotel engineer, a waiter, and a dispatcher.

Her new husband of seven years, "Bonz," is a chef. Since he is from Massachusetts, she calls him "her missionary."

Malihini surfed and fished as a keiki, took up hula at seven, performed on a stage for the first time at 12, graduated from Lahainaluna High School, and began a long career in the tourist industry.

Starting in 1993, she served in a variety of posts at KBH before becoming a full-time concierge—suggesting tours, answering guests' questions, and making dinner reservations. Malihini often comes from behind her concierge desk to teach hula on the lawn three days a week. She also hosts a tour of the property in which she explains the medicinal value of various native plants and even puts on a demonstration on how to cut pineapple.

Before there was a Ka'anapali Beach Resort, Malihini described Lahaina affectionately as being "nice."

"Everywhere you went there were familiar faces. When a child was born into that village, everyone was responsible for that child until they grew up. If you got out of hand, because you are on island, your parents knew it even before you got home," she said. "We were taught to respect everyone." She laments that parents today are not teaching this value.

One of her biggest passions is hula. She regards it as

one of the few things of the past that "we Hawaiians have to hang onto."

Malihini is also admired by her KBH colleagues for her remarkable ability to remember the names of previous guests. The close relationship she has with visitors is seen every day as she "welcomes them home."

MAI-TAI MAN
Dale Simonsen
400,000 Mai-Tai Man

ONE FAN calls him just about the coolest bartender on Maui. Thousands of visitors and locals know him only as Dale—the blue-shirted, congenial, low-key, quick-to-laugh purveyor of drinks at the Tiki Bar at the Ka'anapali Beach Hotel.

Dale Simonsen has a lifetime of observations on changing lifestyles and the habits of both visitors and locals. He's been serving up drinks at the KBH for an amazing 40 years (gulp!)—from Diet Cokes to mai tais, unique concoctions, and everything in between.

Dale is so laid back he is an easy interview, talking in short phrases one morning as he mixed Bloody Mary's and kibitzed with his regular customers, some of whom he has served for at least 25 years. The conversation, recorded on tape complete with sound effects, went something like this:

AUTHOR: Where did you grow up? What did your parents do? Where did you go to school?

DALE: Born in Oahu in 1946. Dad was in the military. Mom was a nurse at Queens (Medical Center).

We came to Maui when I was three years old and lived in a little town called Puʻukoliʻi. I went to Kam III (King Kamehameha III School on Front Street) and graduated from Lahainaluna High School in '64.

I joined the US Army and served at Fort Ord, California. I went to college, but I had to return because my mom (long divorced) hurt her back. Had to pay the bills (laughs). I got a job in construction. I worked on tiling at the Royal Lahaina.

AUTHOR: Did you set tile?

DALE: No, I was a mixer—a mudder (laughs). KBH hired me as a bellman in 1969. I worked nights. I was the low person on the totem pole (laughs). I started at Sugar Mill Lounge inside—on-the-job training. We had lounge music, and then a piano bar, and then went to local trios. The Tiki Bar opened in 1980 near the whale-shaped swimming pool. It replaced the Shipwreck Bar. Looking back, this job was a blessing. My life could have been working in electronics in California. I was very fortunate to be able to stay on Maui.

(Dale met the love of his life at work and figured it was about time he settled down. He married, had two daughters, and was widowed after 20 years.)

AUTHOR: So what drink is your specialty?

DALE: Anything is fine. Almost anything (laughs).

AUTHOR: How have people's drinking habits changed over
        the years?

DALE: In the sixties, it used to be Harvey Wallbangers,
        Tequila Sunrises. In the nineties, it was beer and
        shots and then wine by people who thought they
        were connoisseurs. Word has gotten out about
        our mai tais. We were known for them. We
        also invented drinks. Tommy Rosenthal (Dale's
        longtime partner, mostly working the day shift)
        invented the Lava Flow (rum, piña colada, ice
        cream, and strawberry puree). I invented the
        Ka'anapali Cooler: rum, orange and pineapple
        juices, and blackberry and cherry brandies.

AUTHOR: What about the visitors? How have they
        changed?

DALE: Back in the seventies, people weren't rushed.
        Now they are always planning trips to Hana,
        but it's not long until they come back. People
        like the bar, because they have a bird's-eye view
        of the pool and can watch their kids while they
        have lunch.

AUTHOR: What's the secret to making a good mai tai?
        How many mai tais do you make a day?

DALE: Probably about 40.

AUTHOR: That's 200 mai tais per work week, right? That's

10,000 mai tais a year. (About 10,000 mai tais a year for 40 years adds up to an astounding 400,000 mai tais during a career...and still counting.)
Have you served any famous people?

DALE: Julia Roberts. She played beach volleyball.

AUTHOR: Was Sarah Palin here recently?

DALE: That's right—after Christmas. The paparazzi showed up and she left.

AUTHOR: Did she drink?

DALE: Not that I know of.

AUTHOR: Where do you live?

DALE: I have a house in Lahaina. Bought it in 1971 with my mom; three bedrooms.

CUSTOMER: I'll have a Bud Light.

AUTHOR: What makes a good bartender?

DALE: Show up all the time and early (laughs). You have to be a people person.

AUTHOR: Do you think you qualify?

DALE: I'm working on it. You have to be a psychiatrist,

but I don't give any opinions. It's like Switzerland back here. I am always neutral. If a guest asks what the weather will be, I say, "Well, forecasters often don't get it right. But my theory is it will be windy tomorrow." That way, the bartender doesn't get blamed if the prediction is wrong.

AUTHOR: What do you do when someone is served too much?

DALE: I give them a warning. If they are using foul language and disturbing other guests, this is not acceptable. I don't like to do this when someone is having a good time. But there is a time and place. The third time I say, "This is it," I confiscate their drink. And I give them a choice. I tell them, "I can pick up the phone, or you can leave. It's your choice." The good thing is, this does not happen very often.

AUTHOR: What about the people?

DALE: People love this place. Many come back year after year. You develop a friendship. Sometimes someone doesn't come back for 15 years, and you recognize him.

AUTHOR: Are you good at names?

DALE: Pretty much. But I remember faces. I've met thousands of people.

AUTHOR: So, are you thinking of retiring? Will you walk in with a cane? I won't go that far.

AUTHOR TO A CUSTOMER:

> So, why are you here drinking at 10:00 a.m.? Response heard from across the bar: "Well, it's five o'clock somewhere."

CUSTOMER: I've been coming here since 2006. Dale is the best bartender on the Pacific Rim.

AUTHOR: How do you know that? Have you been to the Pacific Rim? What if there is a better bartender in Tahiti?

CUSTOMER: Well, I have been all over Hawaii. I guess he is the best bartender in Hawaii.

The morning at the bar goes on in similar fashion for a while longer, but you get the idea. In late afternoon, the columnist returns to take photos and meets still more fans of Dale. "He is the best. He is attentive. You don't have to yell at him to get another drink. And he knows what you like," said one.

Susie Johnson of Seattle (everyone at the Tiki Bar last Wednesday seemed to be from the Seattle area) said she has known Dale for 26 years. She said he's heart-warming, caring, and fun. Sharon Henderson chimes in, "Efficiency is good. He is efficient, too. A good word, too."

Another guest had a final word. "You know, Rudy Aquino (before he retired) used to be Mr. Aloha around here. And now Dale is."

HOSTESS SURFER

Laura Blears
Surfer to Hostess with the Mostest

SHE WAS THE FIRST WOMAN in the world to win money in a surfing contest. She posed for a national magazine, leaving little to the imagination. Her illustrious father, Lord James Blears (his real name, not a title) advised her to "go for it."

She was a Smirnoff vodka girl, posing in a white swimsuit on a surfboard for a promotional poster sent to every bar in the islands. She went on ABC's Wide World of Sports, Challenge of the Sexes, as well as its Superstars version, competing with the likes of NFL football star Dick Butkus and others.

She appeared on What's My Line, a popular network show in the eighties, whose panel members had to guess the profession of guests.

Nobody figured out she was a world-class surfer. She is Lahaina's Laura Blears, formerly Laura Blears Chin and Laura Blears Cohn, who has been the "hostess with the mostest" at Kimo's on Front Street for the last 12 of her 31 years there.

"We were trained that you go out with your hands full to tables on the way out of the kitchen and in with your hands full back in," she explained. The years there have flown by because she loves it so much, she said. Eventually, her wrists gave out with carpal tunnel. By now, she believes, she would have been in management if she had not damaged her wrists. "Managers work very hard. They bus tables, bring out dinners, and carry the ice buckets, along with their management duties," she added.

Though Laura completed half of a 100-point training program, she gave it up knowing that her wrists would not handle the strain.

About a decade ago, she put away her server outfit and was named by then-General Manager Ron LaClergue as "Miss Aloha," assigned to rove around tables and chat with diners. She was so good she was moved to the hostess stand, where she has been ever since.

Despite the fact that she is over 60, once a surfer, almost always a surfer. "When I was growing up in Waikiki, it was a magical place," she noted. "As a little girl, I used to surf against the boys, because there were no girl surfers."

When not on boards, Laura, before she was 10, paddled in canoes and rode on catamarans. "My dad brought us over here in the early fifties. We lived right next to Duke's statue on Waikiki Beach on Kalakaua Avenue—now a tony shopping area with a beach (it used to be a beach with some shopping). "It was a two-way street. We were in the old Judge Steiner building.

"It had the very first surf shop in Hawaii underneath. Its owner was a friend and moviemaker. He made Slippery When Wet, one of the first surf movies," Laura said.

"We started surfing when we were little kids. All the beach boys took us out. A few years later, I took my son, Dylan, on a surfboard before he was a year old. The beach boys would take us surfing all the way out to the break. We would stand up with them—even did tandem surfing on top of their shoulders while the man is surfing on the wave. I competed in that when I was 14 years old.

"He surfed in competitions. We all surfed in competitions; it was just a way of life." My dad would say, 'You feel like doing something and it is fun, let's go to do it!'"

Encouraged to surf by her father, Lord James Blears, known to beach boys as Tally Ho, Laura entered her first competition at 12. She lost. To seek comfort, she remembers running to a beach towel shack and crying.

The famous seamstress there was named Take (pronounced Ta-Kay). She used to make all the surfers' shorts. No other surf company made them to order.

Thirty two years ago, surfing in Waikiki, "I ended up being asked by surfing legend Fred Hemmings to enter my very first contest for money. My brother was a finalist in that very first pro contest," she recalled. Laura was an alternate, but the next year she was a real competitor.

"It was billed as '325 men and Laura.' That was the advertising. I beat one guy in my heat, but I never advanced. And I never ended up on the circuit," she said.

Against women, however, she had at least 10 wins mostly gave way to parenting, working and surfing on Maui after she moved here with her first husband, Bonn Chin.

Laura's surfing today is more limited. She still surfs when she can between hosting at Kimo's and teaching water aerobics.

MORNING GODDESS
Alaka'i Paleka
Music Missionary and "Goddess," Too

SHE SAID PIDGIN is her native language and it just comes naturally, but she can also speak the King's English. She once wanted to be a missionary in the Philippines. Some years ago, she was christened "Morning Goddess" by a friend and, despite her reluctance, the nickname stuck.

She is Leslyn Mililani Paleka, for over 22 years KPOA radio's most popular on-air personality.

Better known by her stage moniker, Alaka'i (Ala), the name for the second-in-command at hula schools, the morning deejay and frequent master of ceremonies at local events is number one in morning radio and is heard on the Internet by mainlanders who want their Maui fix.

One of Maui's most charismatic characters—not counting Blackie Gadarian (Voices, July 25, 2008)—Alaka'i insists the goddess nickname should be with a small "g," as to not to offend the one and only God.

Her philosophy of life is best summed up by her voice mail that begins with her singing "We have been blessed with another day," and ends with "Have a blessed day and know that you are loved."

Aspiring to be a missionary from her school days in Paia, where she was mentored by a Filipino missionary, she said she wanted to go to that country to "save them for Jesus."

My charming wife, when told Ala wanted to be a missionary, quipped, "She may not be a missionary, but she's a missionary of music." How true, since she has mentored many local groups.

Ala has known musicians all her life through her father, Danny "Bully" Paleka, a 100 percent Hawaiian who made a living playing piano and operating Maui nightclubs. Musicians were always around; Ala plays the ukulele and a bit of piano.

Danny Paleka met and married his wife (100 percent German) while serving as a US Marine in California. She was a student at USC.

Settling in Maui after marriage, they eventually sent their musically inclined daughter to the prestigious Kamehameha Schools. There she was enmeshed in Hawaiian culture and its musical tradition.

Ala was encouraged to get a degree in police science at Maui Community College—a mistake, she said.

She did serve a stretch as a parole officer in Hilo, where she had moved earlier with her parents.

Describing herself as a Maui girl, Ala moved back to Maui hoping to get a prison job at the county jail. She ended up renovating a house she acquired and hanging out for a year when the county showed no interest in a female guard.

Then, at the suggestion of a friend, she applied for a job the KPOA Lahaina studios. "I started February 5, 1985," she said with precision and has been with the station all but four years since.

As a deejay doubling as a security officer, she began with an afternoon time slot. Her success secret? "I had to learn my craft—to be brash. I showed up and I showed well."

Later, she was switched to a weekend show where she grew popular, and finally to a program from 6:00 a.m. to 10:00 a.m. where she has spun records (and later CDs) for the past 17 years. Today she doubles as KPOA program director.

The goddess is so comfortable on the air that she answers a columnist's questions between commercials, on-air phone calls, and songs, switching between one task and another without pause (written by a guy who sometimes gets nervous in front of a microphone).

When not on the radio, Ala seems to be everywhere as emcee at countless festivals and music gigs, two nights a week at Royal Lahaina Luau, and at charity events.

Ala is so charismatic with her funny patter and quick quips and jibes at musicians, she often gets equal billing—and, it seems, equal time—with them. Eventually, she lets them play.

Asked where her charisma comes from, she ascribed it to "an appreciation of life," noting, "I have a haole mother and a Hawaiian father. Luckily my brain belongs to my mother. She always thought education was the best gift.

"My father was all about aloha. I am fortunate that I have the Hawaiian part. You want to know a lot of different things and be eclectic, but you should always start with love and class and sophistication. That's what I learned from my father."

One of those loves is Maui. "This is one of the few places on earth people really have a passion for. If you are going to live on Maui, you have to have a passion for it."

LEI LADY
Fayth Marciano
Life of a Lei Lady and More

DECKED OUT IN HIGH HEELS, gliding elegantly between tables largely in silence, and wearing smiles and killer dresses below the knees and up to the neckline, the lei ladies of Lahaina leave a trail of wonderful aromas as they go to and fro.

Visitors and locals notice lei lady Michelle Fayth Marciano, known as Fayth Flowers, right away for her good looks and infectious personality.

Fayth is her real middle name. At just five feet, Fayth is an independent contractor, wannabe actress, and singer-songwriter who works for a distributor of leis.

A dozen or so lei ladies bring the beautiful creations to dozens of the better restaurants each night.

The lei lady known as Fayth Flowers places leis on a visitor celebrating her 21st birthday at the Hyatt Regency Maui. The lei was gifted by a friend.

There is something special about Fayth in the same sense as in the 1998 movie Something About Mary starring Cameron Diaz.

Carrying a basket of leis that she picked up from the distributor and replenishing them from the trunk of her car from time to time, she begins one early evening at Mark El-man's Honu and Mala Ocean Tavern, then walks to Aloha Mixed Plate. After a few other stops, she drives to Whalers Village in Ka'anapali.

At each restaurant, the drill is the same: gliding through with a smile, showing her basket mostly in silence (that is the rule). Fayth being Fayth, if she sees a receptive couple, she may ask whether the dinner is a special occasion.

At Maui Fish and Pasta, she sells nary a lei. A short walk to Tropica at the Westin finds a wedding party finishing a meal. Ten leis grace her basket. A customer buys all 10, and Fayth drapes them over the bride's party and little kids.

Leis usually are sold one or two at a time, and Fayth shares the profits. Driving to the Hyatt late (around 9:00 p.m.), she greets the doormen and offers a friendly aloha to a couple in the lobby, complementing the lady wearing a pretty lei.

At Son'z Maui at Swan Court, two couples remain. Ta-blemates from New Jersey, each celebrating three decades of marriage, seem willing to talk. Fayth turns on the charm.

Learning about the anniversaries, she said, "In Hawaiian tradition, it is traditional to exchange leis. You place them heart to heart and seal them with a kiss." Four leis soon adorn the two couples.

Fayth offers to take their pictures with their iPhones (no charge) and talks to them about New Jersey, where her own relatives came from. Then it's off to her last stop, Paradise Grill, before heading home to Wailuku.

The something about Fayth relates to her spirituality. Her uniqueness starts with a rare mix of ancestry (Moroccan, Is-raeli, Polish). After growing up in Florida, after a series of unspecified traumas, she enrolled in California's Santa Mon-ica University to secure a degree in something called spiritual psychology. She then decided spiritual Hawaii would make an ideal home.

A deep thinker, Fayth said she is on a journey "to move to a place that identifies her authentic self, living not based on how she was conditioned, reframing unresolved issues, and being able to choose from the soul's purpose, the heart's desire."

She is fond of saying things like,

"Follow your heart and never ever give up on your dreams."

"Believe in yourself."

"It never hurts to smile too much; no matter how you smile.

"Spiritual growth is a process, not an event."

A certified yoga instructor, Fayth wants to teach other people spirituality through her yoga company called Yoga Fairy. The 29-ish Fayth hopes one day to find her own soul mate and raise a family. "The Universe will bring me the right man at right moment," she said.

Maui is home to a great many remarkable people, a treasure trove for a columnist. Fayth fits in perfectly, partly as a talented seller of leis, but more so because of her spiritual side that cannot be captured very easily in a short space.

On her Facebook page, Fayth describes herself as owner/yoga instructor at the Yoga Fairy and "lover of life + dream."

BIRDMAN
Brian Botka
PURRFECT Days in Paradise

IN THIS ERA of the digital camera—whether a clunky version, handheld, iPhone, or iPad—no visitor or resident, no matter how many sunsets, hula dancers, rainbows, or plumeria photographed this year or in past years, is ever going to beat out Brian Botka for photos taken.

The job of the "birdman of Front Street" Tuesday through Sunday evenings is bringing joy and a permanent record in the form of photographs of people with parrots to thousands of customers. For 20 years, Brian has happily worked for a company originally formed three decades ago by one Bud "the Birdman" Clifton.

Brian is much more than a casual clicker of a camera. An artist and accomplished photographer in his own right, the birdman selects from five multicolored parrots, macaws, and cockatoos that he perches on hands and shoulders of customers. On customers go silk leis just the right color to match what they are wearing. Brian snaps away, finally proclaiming, "purrfect ."

Listen in as he talks to both birds and customers, his usual street patter beginning with, "Come on up. They won't poop on you on my shift—guaranteed."

Brian, to a new customer: "Hey…hold my little baby, lay 'em down. Now what I am going to do is a few different shots. We will put Mai Tai (the youngest parrot at 30) on you. His not going to goober on you.

"Don't show fear, people; they sense fear. Now I am going to put a bird on your head. He wants to be top dog today. Oh, this is going to be beautiful. I want that chin forward," he tells a lady on the left.

To the bird Mai Tai: "Preen her hair, make her look good," Botka watches the parrot gently grab thin strands of his customer's hair. "Good boy."

To the customer: "Don't worry about a thing. You are looking good." To the bird Mai Tai: "Mai Tai, look at the camera. Peanut, look at the camera, man. On one, two, three…" (Click).

To the customers: "That's excellent. Stay with me. I want

to see your teeth. This is a photo you will want to see forever. Awesome. One, two, two-and-a-half, three, big smile…This is a phenomenal shot. Got it. Purrfect, excellent job, very well done."

Brian puts birds on a tiny baby, a three-year-old with a toothy smile, and a parade of family groups, among them "one poor guy" who was here with six older sisters.

Over the years at the parrots' perch near the corner of Pioneer Inn facing the public library, Brian's film and digital camera lenses have captured everyone from celebrities to a group of two dozen cheerleaders here for a contest at the Hyatt all in one frame.

Actor Dustin Hoffman one time brought back from Lahaina a parrot picture and added a painting from artist Jim Kingwell for good measure.

Carlos Santana and his new wife have been in. So have movie stars Demi Moore, Danny DeVito, and Arnold Schwarzenegger. And even President Bill Clinton's political consultant James "It's the economy, stupid" Carville.

A bit of a political junkie himself—his brother works in Washington—Brian engaged Carville in a memorable four-hour marathon conversation right on Front Street. He also got a hug from Mary Matalin, the conservative wife of the "Ragin' Cajun," who he said was the sweetest, smartest person he had met for a long time.

Joking with clients in ways that bring automatic smiles, Brian says "purrfect" so often when he looks through the lens that one bird, noted it well. One day, the bird spontaneously began crying out "purrfect" all day. Tiring quickly of the gambit, the parrot hasn't returned to using the word since.

Brian points out that parrots are one of the oldest creatures on earth. "They are telepathic and very intelligent," he says. "They work on a higher frequency and notice things I would never notice." Birds know enough not to eat all the fruit on a tree. Humans will and later they will starve. The birds are purchased from breeders. Though he often kisses them on the beak, he has never been bitten.

In the early days, he used film—so much that a photo store set up a branch right in Pioneer Inn to process photos overnight ($60,000 worth of prints a year). Today he uses a $2,000 digital camera. The results from the photographer continue to be "purrfect" every time.

THREE
TODAY'S HAWAIIANS and THEIR CULTURE

My goal is to educate people so they know the preciousness of what makes Hawaii and Maui separate from the rest of the world and we have something to offer during these turbulent years.

—Ed Lindsey

Cultural Advisor Clifford Naeʻole in Hawaiian garb.

KUPUNA
Ed Lindsey
Passing to a New 'Aina

YOU CAN NEVER TELL a person's complete heritage through looks. Kupuna and spiritual leader Ed Lindsey had the look of a malihini possibly because he was descended from a New England sea captain. Lindsey even was given a Christian first name, an irony since his core heritage was Hawaiian.

Hawaiians gave their children Christian names frequently in the last century because their culture was not looked on favorably by many who were not born Hawaiian.

Yet Lindsey was Hawaiian through and through. A graduate of the prestigious Kamehameha Schools (founded by a Hawaiian royalty and once open only to Hawaiians), the solidly built man began focusing more on his heritage after retiring from teaching. Passionate about giving back to the land he loved, Lindsey began restoration work on an ancient valley and said, "people need to work together for this island."

Hawaiians love to "talk story," (engaging in good conversation). Talking story under a shade tree, sitting on a wooden bench nine years before he passed away, the respected elder waxed a bit clairvoyant, noting that "you will be remembered for what you have done in life. At your wake, your survivors will get 20 minutes to say what your life meant."

When Ed succumbed at 70, the survivors at the celebration of his life needed much longer than 20 minutes to celebrate.

In a eulogy, he was described as "a Hawaiian warrior." The pride and joy of this man of aloha was Honokai Valley.

Lindsey remembers when Lahaina was a typical plantation town of mom-and-pop shops. "Now what we have are cookie-cutter shops going after visitor money," he lamented. "We had a stronger sense of community then and bonds of friendship. Today we have people rushing around stalled in traffic."

Lindsey's sorrow was that too many regard Maui as simply "a playground, a Disneyland" where newcomers don't meet local people. They come in and move away "like tumbleweeds."

"My goal," this inspiring leader said, "is to educate people so they know the preciousness and what makes Hawaii and Maui separate from the rest of this world, and we have something to offer during these turbulent years."

Two things Lindsey would especially like from malihini are more interest in discovering the richness of Hawaiian culture and more respect for Hawaiian values centered on the 'aina, or land. This includes the spiritual side as well as the Hawaiian heritage.

He noted that Hawaiians have always been quick to adjust to new styles of living. The monarchs supported the building of the first high school (then equivalent to college) west of the Mississippi, and Iolani Palace in Honolulu had telephones and electricity before the White House.

One of the culture's most important philosophies revolves around pono (doing the right thing). Kupuna believe one of the most important right things, Lindsey said, "should be fighting for quality of life, and that will benefit everybody and not just somebody walking in here and making a ton of money and walking out. You do not take our abundant resources for your own personal gain."

Although he believes entrepreneurs are learning, "when you start digging away at the layers of this onion, you look at the bottom, you see dollar signs. Is it cost effective? How can we bump up profits? It is important to keep these local companies healthy—but not unbridled. It's a two-way street."

The privilege of listening to Ed Lindsey, as he sat on a wooden bench came to an end with much left unsaid.

Years after this was first written, the power of the man leaps from the page. From Lindsey and so many others, the author has learned a lot, forming a new appreciation for Lindsey as the years have passed, for he was a very wise man.

At community meetings, people are not hesitant to proclaim their views. Lindsey would just sit back and listen. And then at the end, he would stand up and put it all into perspective. And it is still good advice: to do something good for the community.

CULTURAL ADVISOR
Clifford Naeʻole
Open the Gate and Come to the Ritz

WHEN THE ANNUAL CELEBRATION OF ARTS officially opens each year at the entrance to the Ritz-Carlton in Kapalua, Kanaka Maoli and resort cultural advisor Clifford Naeʻole takes center stage. The festival planned by Naeʻole is a must-attend annual event for anyone who wants an introduction or continuing education in Hawaiian culture.

A spiritual sunrise ceremony at 5:30 a.m. on a Friday welcomes the day. Later, hula will be performed. Hawaiians will demonstrate ancient crafts. Kupuna in full regalia will offer opening prayers. Stimulating 90-minute discussions will take place on everything from the sensual meanings in hula to tourism and culture.

One of only four resort cultural advisors in the state,

Naeʻole has a heritage that uniquely qualifies him for the job. Some 210 years ago, a Naeʻole ancestor was a warrior king so trusted by Hawaiian royalty that he was charged with bringing up the future great King Kamehameha I, uniter of the Hawaiian Islands. Yet the usually mild mannered, now spiritual Clifford almost turned his back on his own culture.

Growing up near Waiheʻe, north of Wailuku, on the taro fields farmed by his grandfather and father, Naeʻole remembers running through taro patches and picking huge sweet guava off the trees, playing in the mud and having fun while his hardworking parents did the tough work of putting food on the table.

After graduation from high school in Wailuku, Clifford was taken aside by his grandfather and told it was time for Kou Manawa, your turn as a hiapo (the first born) to continue the legacy of farming.

Clifford refused, aspiring to be a travel agent—an idea he later abandoned—and took off for the good life in California, where he married a lady from England. "Why did I marry her? Because," he joked, remembering his royal heritage, "England still has a king and queen."

When Naeʻole left Maui, he was told by his grandfather, "You've chosen to dine on the buffet of life." Coming back after 12 years, Clifford said, "the table was empty.

"The land was lost. It really hit hard, but what I have accomplished since would make my grandfather proud."

Naeʻole sought to find his culture, starting with hula lessons, then language and chants, and finally embracing Hawaiian spirituality.

"My son was enrolled in a Hawaiian language immersion school. One day he asked for help with his homework. His textbook was written in Hawaiian. I spoke zero. I knew aloha and mahalo and that was it," he explained. This is the man whose voice mail today starts and ends with Hawaiian. (Incidentally, he now considers himself a Kanaka Maoli—one, in his definition, who lives the old culture.)

Clifford's renaissance—a work in progress, much like today's Hawaiian Renaissance of things cultural—is still underway because he says he still has much to learn.

Hired by the Ritz-Carlton as a telephone operator two weeks before the resort opened in 1992, Clifford took inspiration from the *iwi*, the bones of 2,000 Hawaiians whose discovery and preservation led legendary landowner Colin Cameron to move the location of his hotel. Pushing the general manager to do even more by the culture, Clifford was quickly promoted to full-time cultural advisor—as he puts it, "the best job in the world."

"As cultural advisor, I have the opportunity to create bridges to reconnect the host culture to those we host (our visiting guests). I serve as the link between the Hawaiian community and the hotel on things cultural," he noted. This ranges from little things like correcting spelling of Hawaiian words on menus to supporting Aloha Festivals and this weekend's free Celebration of the Arts.

"Our purpose," he continued, "is to help visitors and those who live here understand our culture better through the lure of art, intellectual discussion, panels, films, and music.

"There will be a timely discussion of timely topics but no confrontation. Say to people what you believe, we tell panelists, but listen to others' points of view."

Naeʻole notes that Hawaiians "want understanding of who we are and what we can become and understanding of the injustices that have been done and continue to this day.

"I am not a Hawaiian according to law. This hurts me deeply. You are a Native Hawaiian with a capital N and capital H only if you have 50 percent Hawaiian blood, and I do not." Clifford added, "Those who are born here and choose to live here are part of the solution. If you are living in a gated community, the question is, are you keeping people out, or are you keeping yourself in? You worked hard and you deserve what you have but don't lock yourself out. My job is to tell a story and get someone to tell that story to someone else."

KUMU HULA
Hokulani Holt
What Makes Hawaii, Hawaii

"IT IS TIME FOR ALL OF US to stop and reflect upon all the great aspects that make these Hawaiian Islands so special. We need to slow down and get back to the basics," noted Clifford Nao'ele at the annual Celebration of the Arts. One of many speakers did just that.

Hokulani Holt, renowned kumu hula, grandmother, language specialist, and cultural programs director of the Maui Arts & Cultural Center provided her own version of the basics by telling a charming, funny story well worth repeating. Her talk, "Kuleana of Aloha," went beyond a common use of kuleana (taking care of the land) to a more fundamental meaning: taking care of and respecting people.

Those unfamiliar with kuleana think this is an amazing thing, she explained. "It means responsibility and accountability. What this tells us is we are held accountable for the things we do.

"If you were raised in a Hawaiian household, you know this from day one. You do this not because someone is watching, but especially when someone is not watching."

Holt said her three children have *kuleana* in their lives. "My oldest sister lives in San Francisco, never been married, has no children. We are her only *'ohana* (family), so to my number two, my son Lono, she is his *kuleana*. When she gets old, his *kuleana* is to take care of Aunty.

"My younger daughter has me as her *kuleana*. This is the daughter; when I get old, she gotta take care of me. My other daughter, the eldest—and such is the life of the eldest—her *kuleana* is the whole family, the welfare of her brother and sister, her nieces, and any children. Her kuleana is to make sure everybody is cool.

"You start when they are young—six, seven, eight, nine. Now they are in their twenties, nearly 30, so kuleana is a natural part of their life.

"Kuleana sometimes is seen by others as being burdensome, but its other definition is that it is a privilege. Think of all the times they took care of you. If you look at kuleana not only as a responsibility but a privilege, (you practice) it to the highest standard possible.

"In ancient Hawaii, this standard was very important. We lived right on the beach and we used to lay nets. The job of keiki was to clean the limu (seaweed) off the nets after fishing. You'd sit in the yard and go over them inch by inch. Clean the net, repair the net, dry the net, and bring it back to the net house and ready to go, because if the fish started running, you grab the net and got to go. If your holes were not patched when you took the net out, you are not going to catch fish. And who suffers? Everybody."

By high school, Holt said teenagers are likely to complain that concepts of *kuleana* and adherence to rules are old fashioned. Holt told her own children, "This is not a choice; there are many choices in life, but not these."

The same holds true, she said, for aloha—the love and

compassion deep inside, at whose heart is the Golden Rule: "Do unto others as you would have others do unto you."

"It's what makes grandparents take care of their grandchildren, and grandchildren take care of their grandparents. You give aloha to others, you receive aloha. It's a cycle; aloha is given and returned, though not always directly. You do not just take, take, take."

Holt acknowledges that keiki learning to follow the rules sometimes require "a whack or two." She told the audience that "if you are in childhood education, sorry, but this works."

In each generation, she noted, "Hawaiians who follow cultural tradition get a little more lenient. Yet a good many Hawaiians still bring up keiki in the old ways. The evidence is there every day: friendly greetings and willingness to help, genuine affection shown with a kiss, sharing and giving, like Uncle George Kahumoku gifting anyone who visits him with vegetables from his farm. Unfortunately, not everyone who has grown up or lives here follows these lessons. Young thugs beat up strangers, or there's yelling at visitors over trivial matters like choice beach parking stalls."

Kuleana, responsibility, respect, aloha. That's what makes Hawaii, Hawaii. We all win when we see it, lose when we don't.

HAWAIIANS
Malihini Keahi-Heath
David Kapaku
Flag Flap Goes to Core of Hawaiian Issues

WHEN A LOCAL ARTIST was asked to fashion a logo to promote the display of fireworks for a July 4 celebration in Lahaina, she decided instead to create a painting called

"Inspiration Celebration." This sparked dinnertime conversation in Hawaiian households and bothered some *Kanaka Maoli*. Art can be provocative to the beholder and spur debate, and so it has been with this painting.

To highly respected Hawaiians Kahu David Kapaku, whose ancestors have been here 900 years, and whose great-grandfather was a feather bearer for the king, the flag flap goes to the core of Hawaiian issues.

According to Kapaku, as well as a short film shown at the burial place of Kamehameha on the island of Hawaii, today's state flag with Britain's Union Jack in the corner is identical—except for an extra stripe—to the flag Kamehameha I approved as the official flag of the kingdom in the early 1800s. That flag was the successor to an older one featuring a *kahili* (royal standard) and paddles to represent Hawaiians' connection with the sea.

The first post-contact flag, influenced by the arrival of the British, had the Union Jack surrounded by an all red field. There was a time when Hawaiians raised the British flag when the Brits were in port and the Stars and Stripes when the Americans were here. Each side became upset when they saw the other country's flag flying.

To placate both sides—perhaps as a smart political move—today's flag incorporating both the Union Jack and the Stars and Stripes was approved by the king as the official Hawaiian flag.

Thus, it could be argued this "Kamehameha flag" is worthy of respect for the last 150 years. Yet, when Heath first saw a painting with parts of the American flag and a small Hawaiian flag in the middle, she was offended. If it was the other way around, with the big flag Hawaiian and the American little, she said that "maybe I would have thought differently."

"This painting is controversial," Kapaku declared, "because of the issue of statehood. The Hawaiian flag can be considered a symbol of colonialism by hard nosed members of the sovereignty movement."

Kapaku pointed out that the Apology Bill passed by Congress and signed by President Clinton officially apologizes to the Hawaiian people for the illegal overthrow of its government.

"If someone stole your car, it was taken illegally. But don't you still actually own the car? You look at this painting, and you are going to see people disagreeing with the fact that we are part of the United States. By this logic, 'stolen' Hawaii does not belong to the United States," Kapaku said.

Most of the flag discussion focused on Hawaiians' loss of land, the core value of Hawaiian life for centuries and still the subject of reverence.

"We Hawaiians are considered a minority here," Keahi-Heath declared. "Our issues are huge." Hawaiians had paperwork showing they owned certain land for decades, if not centuries, she explained. Yet under Hawaii law, if land is unoccupied, it can be claimed by anyone who declares it as his or her own and pays overdue taxes.

Much of the land "owned" by the island's largest corporations was secured through a procedure called adverse possession. Sugar growers grabbed water rights. Hawaiians, whose lives were dominated by crops to sustain themselves, left adjoining lands, because streams dried up and they could no longer grow anything. So they left the land, making it vulnerable to takeover.

Growers, according to Keahi-Heath, abused the land, then decided, after a period of years, to abandon it, discontinuing crops and growing them elsewhere.

"They abused the land so harshly, we can't go back and grow what we used to grow," she commented.

"Our land issues," Keahi-Heath added, "are even fought in court on another island," transferred there to discourage testimony of Maui people who would have to travel off-island on short notice.

On land that families once owned, "we sometimes get challenged that we are trespassing. This is what hurts. Others have dominion over part of the land that once belonged to our ancestors," Keahi-Heath added.

"Despite these differences," she stressed, "we respect the Hawaiian flag. But the little Hawaiian flag in the artwork is a symbol of our turmoil. For generations, we have been trying to be heard."

Summing up, Kapaku said, "When I see the smaller Hawaiian flag, it makes me feel other people are still in charge of my destiny.

"We are called the host culture, but we have not hosted anything since 1893. What are we hosting when we are not the dominant culture?

"For me, it feels like I am being imprisoned within the borders of the United States. Everything I believe in as a Hawaiian is being stripped. My space is getting smaller, because everything is being stripped of me. That box (of the Hawaiian flag in the painting) makes me very claustrophobic."

If art promotes discussion and debate, so be it. On an island peopled by full-blooded Hawaiians, Filipinos, Portuguese, Japanese, *hapas* (part white), and new arrivals, we all gain by lending a sympathetic ear to the voices of this land's Kanaka Maoli. If, that is, we would only listen.

HAWAIIAN
David Kapaku
Pondering the Hawaiian God Ku and Church

GROWING UP IN HONOKOWOHAU VALLEY descended from a long line of *Kahuna* (priests) who paid tribute to *Ke Akua* (God), Kahu David Kapaku knew at five years old he wanted to be a man of God. His grandfather named him David for the biblical figure whose linage is traced to Jesus.

During 12 years of college religious studies, Kahu David *(kahu* means minister) pondered the relationship between Christianity and Hawaiian spirituality.

Hawaiians worshipped Ku Nui Akea (symbolizing stateliness and balance); Lono Nui Akea (the God of fertility), who Native Hawaiians believed returned in the form of Captain Cook in 1778; and Kane Nui Akea (symbolizing life).

Christians have a Holy Trinity—the Father, Son, and Holy Ghost—and Hawaiians their own Trinity in the form of Ku, Lono, and Kane. Hawaiians thought their three deities represented the one, true God.

David noted that it is "kind of sad that Christianity has not embraced many of the spiritual aspects of Hawaiians."

When the missionaries arrived, they found a fertile field among *Kanaka Maoli* (Native Hawaiians) who were already spiritual. Because spiritual Hawaiians didn't know Jesus or God the Father, their concepts of spirituality early on were never embraced, David believes.

Hawaiian tradition includes stories of the flood (40 days and 40 nights). Christ judges believers at the pearly gates. In Hawaiian tradition, Ku is also regarded as a judge, seeking to keep things in balance.

Ku often is considered a god of war. When land is snatched

away from people unjustly, it is Ku who is looked upon to achieve balance and go to war to give it back.

According to Kahu David, some Hawaiians still believe in the old gods, including Madame Pele (lua pele is the Hawaiian term for volcano) who symbolizes land and its creation.

To Hawaiians, land is more important than people, with reverence for land still a driving force today.

"People come and go. The land is forever," many Hawaiians believe. Hawaiian lands, especially Iao Valley and Honolua Bay, are considered sacred not because blood was shed there, but because both were the site of places of worship (heiau temples).

There are an estimated 1,500 *heiau* sites on Maui and 1,500 sacred places, most of them still unidentified.

Kahu David preaches Christian theology, but at the same time he seeks to keep alive those Hawaiian spiritual traditions that he believes are fully in tune with Christianity.

Every Friday, he and his Indiana-born wife, Kenda, sell baskets they make in their home in Honokohau Valley to visitors at the Westin Maui.

They weave them in part to keep in touch with Hawaiian tradition. David plays the ukulele, sells the baskets, and frequently engages his customers in conversation about his most important mission: spreading the word of God.

KAPAKU REVISITED
David Kapaku
Love of the Land Is Paramount

"IF YOU LOVE MAUI, you have a responsibility to learn as much as you can," declared Kahu David Kapaku. Sitting in beautiful Honokohau Valley, where his direct relatives settled 900 years ago, Kapaku, a minister of the Ka'ahumanu Church and holder of bachelor's, master's, and doctorate degrees in religious studies, has powerful stories to tell.

What this smart, perceptive son of the North Shore has to say about change sweeping the island, development, Hawaiian traditions, Christianity, and mythical gods offers anyone curious about this place much food for thought.

Hawaii has long been a magnet for newcomers, setting up a clash between new and old. When Tahitians migrated to the Big Island 10 centuries ago and changed the religion, they enlisted thousands of Hawaiians to carry two million pounds of rocks 20 miles to build more elaborate heiau (places of worship) for human sacrifice. The Makihous, the family name on his mother's side, wanted none of this and fled to Hana on Maui.

Later, they traveled far around the coast to the most beautiful spot they could find: Honokohau Valley. Kapaku's great-great-great-grandfather fought with King Kamehameha I's warriors in the bloody battle of Iao Val

Much later, Chinese immigrants came to their valley to help with pineapple. And then came resorts and people arriving on jets. Some of the newcomers assimilated, and some didn't.

"There are people who have been here 40 years who still do not understand Hawaiians or our traditions," Kapaku observed. "Thirty years ago, when people came to live here, they adapted.

"People wanted to surf, just hang out. Now it is all business. 'How can I make money off this condo and sell it for twice as much?'

"Today they have to have a big house and want Maui to be like California.

Yet there is still a Hawaii where you can hear the wind,

you can hear the flowing water.

"This is what people imagine Hawaii to be. But some say, 'I need more money. I will put a house here. I will build another house there. I will cover this whole area all the way to Olowalu.' It's insanity," he said.

"People who first come here have a dream of what it would be like," he said. Visitors the minister meets are disappointed. "They say, 'I think Maui is beautiful,' but they have old pictures in their minds that Maui is a balmy place. They come and see a Costco, they see a Walmart, and say they were not expecting that. This change is very disturbing.

"It's disappointing to see very expensive homes that no one is living in—$10 million, $15 million, and no one is there. The greatest disappointment is to see the Hawaiian people having to leave because they can't afford to live here. I tell people, 'If you went to China, would you expect to see Chinese? If you come to Hawaii, would you expect to see Hawaiians?' Visitors are surprised to learn the percentage of Hawaiians on Maui is small. The typical reaction is, 'Are you kidding me?'"

For Hawaiians, love of the land is paramount. This love is shared by many newcomers. "The first thing people see when they come here is the beauty. The unfortunate thing is, that is not all there is to see.

"When you fall in love, you want to know everything. And you begin to learn about (Hawaiians). You see a tree and it is beautiful. But there is more beauty under the surface if you could see the whole thing," he explained.

CULTURAL HISTORIAN
Hinano Rodrigues
Preserving Maui

HINANO IS MY TEACHER. And as he puts it to students of his Hawaiian language and second culture class at Maui Community College's new West Side Education Center in Lahaina, "you will always be my students." If you spend 20 minutes a day, seven days a week, during the course and haven't learned Hawaiian, he said he will tutor you later for free.

What one is humbled by is how complex and how different Hawaiian cultural values are from western values. For this writer and most readers committed to being enriched by the experience, this shapes up as an endless journey of discovery, given its many nuances, with no end in sight.

Hinano Rodrigues—three-eighths Hawaiian, three-eighths Japanese, and two-eighths Portuguese, raised as a Hawaiian—is descended from great-great-great-great-grandfather Kamakakehau, who was summoned by King Kamehameha I to Ukumehame to serve as *konohiki* (head overseer) of the king's cattle.

One-day-old Hinano joined the traditional Hawaiian system of hanai and was sent off for his first five years to be brought up by his grandmother, Louise Leialoha Kaahui, to learn Hawaiian ways. And every weekday, his real mother, Adeline KUMUileolihau Kaahui-Rodrigues, would journey from Wailuku to the new "dream city" of Kahului to visit him.

In this manner, the strong *'ohana* (bonds that Hawaiians live by were created with young Hinano tied closely to his grandmother (really a second mother) for life. Through daily contact between birth mother, son, and surrogate mother, the three generations formed a never-to-be-broken bond.

After schooling at Wailuku Elementary and Iao Intermediate, Rodrigues was off to Honolulu and Kamehameha Schools and the University of Hawaii. During his sophomore year in high school, Hinano had—like a number of others—an epiphany after reading Hawaii's Story by Hawaii's Queen, the autobiography of Queen Lili'uokalani and her account of her overthrow by the US government. Right then, Hinano decided to learn much more about Hawaiian culture.

Only 2,000 people across the islands, most over 65, could speak Hawaiian when his learning started. The language was dying, Hinano said. So he took two years of high school Hawaiian and four years in college (one of only three in his senior school class to study the language).

Back on Maui in 1975, Hinano became the first teacher of Hawaiian at Maui Community College (MCC). After a 20-year detour to California to get a law degree—his second epiphany was that law might be the answer to overturning court decisions that trampled Hawaiians' rights to the land—Hinano was called back home in 2005 to keep a series of family promises after a mainland career in state government and the private sector.

The Olowalu Lanakila Hawaiian Protestant Church chapel had burned to the ground in 1930. Sugar planters cut off water at his ancestral home's *taro* patch in Ukumehame in 1945 and the plants withered and lay dormant for 50 years. Hinano and his parents set to work. Today, water flows, the taro is growing, and plans to rebuild the chapel are underway.

This is an activity for weekends. Monday to Friday, Hinano works as the only cultural historian on Maui for the state Department of Land and Natural Resources. Monday and Tuesday evenings, this dedicated cultural specialist teaches language and history courses at the new community college branch on the Lahaina side of Cannery Mall.

Truly a son of the land, Hinano has much to say about development, especially since his ancestral home sits amid what would be a planned new town in Olowalu. What this cultural historian fighting to preserve Hawaiian traditions says about development is a real eye-opener for all who struggle with this question. Here Hinano is quoted in full:

"Stopping development is like trying to blot out the sun. It is not an alternative. It is not going to happen. We live in a capitalistic world. Capitalism snowballs. You cannot stop it. What we need to do is to have controlled development. We need to find a balance. This is a hard thing to do.

"Standing on the road and holding a sign is not a solution. The other side gets everything they wanted and you get nothing you wanted. And the development will go through. Say that a Hawaiian wants to stop development. Where does her husband work? He works for a construction company. No development will mean he will lose his job," he continued.

"It used to be that a developer would say, 'This is what I am going to do.' Now, it is turned around. We say, 'So this is what you want to do.' Now it is both sides coming together. I truly believe we should permit development only when developers can prove that they have water. Water is a limited resource on this island."

As valuable as his insights on development may be, even more valuable is what he teaches about five great Hawaiian values. What are they? As Hawaiians say, *a hui hou* until later we meet again.

RODRIGUES REVISITED
Hinano Rodrigues

THE BEACH IS SPECIAL. Green mountainsides and beautiful lands are special. Birds singing at dusk and flowering trees blooming are special. For those who choose to look—locals and visitors—there are those who are more special: Hawaiians, sometimes called Native Hawaiians, perhaps more accurately described as *Kanaka Maoli*. These special people, according to cultural historian Hinano Rodrigues, believe in five things:

Aloha. Aloha is not simply a greeting for hello or good morning. Aloha is compassion. Aloha comes from within, a belief that every person deserves to be treated fairly, honestly, and with sensitivity all the time. Aloha is pronounced with quick flourish. It is not, as so many entertainers and presides at meetings proclaim: alooooo—ha. Aloha, mispronounced, degrades its meaning.

Mana. Hawaiian chiefs had more mana than anyone else. Upon death, their *mana* remained in their bones. Chiefs were buried in secret places so no one could dig up the bones and acquire their *mana.*

Today, these bones can appear almost anywhere soil is turned, and their presence is one of the reasons Hinano and the State Historic Preservation Agency is required to make decisions at least 20 times a year on Maui to decide whether bones found inadvertently—Native Hawaiian or non-Native Hawaiian and more than 50 years old—can be moved or stay in place and what, if anything, can be built over them.

Mana is power. Mana is the power within to create positive change. Every ali'i, every Hawaiian, everyone who lives here or visits, has *mana* to one degree or another. The challenge is to put *mana* to good use. Mana is the power to set the tone of relationships.

Mana can also be regarded as charisma, something people say President Jack Kennedy had and what KPOA radio star Alaka'i Paleka has in abundance. Name your charismatic character. One example of mana: your willingness to smile at someone. Check the reaction.

Niele, meaning you are too inquisitive. Hawaiians abhor the idea of asking questions just as husbands who are lost in their cars do. Even today, some think the reasons those brought up here don't ask questions at meetings is because of *niele.* Hawaiian inquisitiveness involves learning by observing, not asking.

Maha'oi, meaning intrusiveness Hawaiians ask permission for everything they do. Can I pick mangoes from your tree on Saturday? A Hawaiian's usual generous response is "sure." But do not assume permission is endless. Want to pick mangoes next Saturday? Ask again. Or better yet, Hinano jokes, "plant your own tree."

Pono, or balance. Live your life with balance and righteousness and with moderation. When things are out of balance, put them back in balance. For this to be column *pono,* more has to be said. There is no one Hawaiian and no single stereotype. Some Hawaiians embrace aloha, some don't. Some like nothing better than to find an "American" who appreciates the culture, the *'aina* and aloha.

Others remain hostile to those they believe descended from people who took away their land and their kingdom. A few do authentic, traditional hula, most don't.

Hawaiians, we are reminded, are doctors, lawyers, legislators, entertainers, cooks, and auto mechanics. And some Hawaiians are in jail, all too many alienated, discouraged, and distraught.

The best we can all do is to seek understanding, embrace

some of the values, and try a little harder to live aloha and strive to be pono.

ACTIVIST
Charles Maxwell Sr.
Marrying a Smart Girl Makes the Difference

GETTING TO KNOW A HAWAIIAN is not always easy for the newcomer. At a community meeting, awhile back a good number of Hawaiians—but not all—protested in anger, as they believed the graves of their ancestors would be desecrated with construction of a new road. Whether this is true is unclear.

Earlier that day, by chance, this columnist met with Uncle Charlie Maxwell (Kahu Charles Kauluwehi Maxwell Sr.) to do what Hawaiians have done for generations: exchange ideas ("talk story" is the popular phrase).

Before reviewing some of the issues, this cultural practitioner told a tale that sheds important light on what Hawaiians have faced that still shapes what they say and do today. Known like so many as "Uncle" because every Hawaiian is often considered to be related to every other Hawaiian, Maxwell led an early childhood less remarkable than it was typical. The conversation is repeated here at length.

Now a Native Hawaiian activist, priest, spiritual advisor, and self-described cultural practitioner, Maxwell was born on the western tip of Maui in Napili more than 70 years ago. He went to school in the fifties.

His great-great-great-great-grandmother had rights to ancestral lands that stretched all the way from Iao Valley near present-day Wailuku to the Ma'alaea isthmus that links two of Maui's dormant volcanoes.

These substantial lands have been long lost to the descendants of missionaries. (Incidentally, whether the influences of missionaries on Maui and the islands have been good or bad remains a topic of vigorous debate even today.)

Speaking Hawaiian at home, Maxwell lived in Kula on the slopes of Maui's great volcano Haleakala. There he found his early school years extremely challenging, to say the least. "I had a hard time going to school," he said. "I had to stand in the corner. I didn't know what a lightbulb was. We were scolded when we used Hawaiian words. It was very difficult to read an English book; I didn't understand English."

Hearing the old rhyme, "Jack and Jill went up the hill to fetch a pail of water," Maxwell said he did not know what a pail or a hill was, let alone fetch. "I just read it; I didn't know what it meant. I knew it had to do something with *wai* (water)," he explained. Comprehension was zero. This is a problem with generations of Hawaiians. "We don't use English words at home—just broken English. My grades were so bad I became a clown (to endear himself to teachers).

"All the teachers liked me. Rebecca Raymond was my fifth-grade teacher; she took special interest in me and I learned my times tables. After that, everybody ignored me and I forgot it all," he said.

When he graduated from eighth grade, a teacher told him, "If I was you, I would marry a smart girl." And so he did. "I was spoiled. As soon as I got to 13, my father said, 'I am sending you to Lahainaluna (the first high school west of the Rocky Mountains, founded by missionaries), because you are going to be a man.' For one year I cried," Maxwell recalled.

The freshman then underwent a kind of hazing. "Later, I wanted to do to the freshmen what they had done to me. I became *kolohe* (naughty). When I was a junior, I had 500 or

600 hours (of detention), so I quit school," he said.

Dropping out, he could easily have wound up like thousands of his Hawaiian brothers and sisters with lost self-esteem, who make up a large portion of today's prison population.

Instead he went to Baldwin High School and soon met the love of his life: a pretty 17-year-old who went on to become one of this island's leading kumu *na hula* (hula teachers). Luckily for Charles, she also happened to wind up class valedictorian.

Charles had met "the smart girl" he was told to find four years before. He recounts that his future wife, Nina, came up to him and said, "'Oh, you are so luscious.' That night, I went to a football game and found out she was a cheerleader. She waved.

Her father knew my father well. By the time we finished our senior year, we were deeply in love," he said. "So my father said, 'You want to marry that girl? Go ahead—you come live with me.' I had no job, nothing. Everybody said that it wouldn't last, and it lasted one month short of 50 years." (Charlotte Ann "Nina" Maxwell, once a lead dancer for the revered Emma Sharpe, passed away two years ago.)

"I went to work as a laborer, and one day the boss told me, 'you do not have to come back tomorrow.'" Thanks to an uncle, Maxwell was accepted by the Maui Police Department.

"Every case I was on the road, I would call my wife because I never knew how to spell or type. For three months she typed all my reports, and then she made a mistake. They made me correct one sentence and it took me two hours," Maxwell said. So his sergeant told him, "If you don't learn in three months you are out." So the smart girl taught him to type (at 100 words a minute). Fifteen years later, a prisoner crushed both of his knees. And this put him on the road to becoming a Hawaiian activist.

ACTIVIST REVISITED
Charles Maxwell Sr.
Uncle's 35-Year Fight for Hawaiians

AFTER READING HAWAII'S STORY BY HAWAII'S QUEEN, Queen Liliuokalani's vivid account of the overthrow of the Hawaiian Kingdom by US armed forces in 1893, cultural practitioner and Kahu (Rev.) Charles Kauluwehi Maxwell Sr. of Pukalani had no doubt he should become an activist.

Hawaiians needed to fight to regain their lands and rededicate themselves to preserving their fast-disappearing culture of spirituality and aloha. Since 1975, his quest for justice has brought Maxwell to Washington, DC, and the White House, to sacred burial sites at Honokahua Bay and to the valleys of Kahoʻolawe, where Hawaiians were once forbidden to enter.

In Washington, Maxwell pulled no punches with influential senators while explaining the need to recognize Native Hawaiian rights and protect ancient burial grounds.

Dressed in an aloha shirt while his colleagues wore suits, Maxwell told senators he doubted that many even knew Native Hawaiians existed. Frustrated with the conversation, as the kupuna (elder) tells it, he stood up and pounded the table.

"You speak in a language that I don't understand. You are talking about my island," he said. "Everything went quiet. After that, I got invited to all kinds of places—the Oval Office (of the President) and the Rose Garden (at the White House)."

Testifying before Congress, Napili-born Maxwell told how revered *iwi kupuna,* ancestral bones closely connected with Hawaiian spirituality, had been bulldozed and desecrated while preparing the original site of the Ritz-Carlton, Kapalua. Native Americans, present in full regalia, cried in sorrow and empathy when they heard his story.

In the end, Uncle Charlie and his colleagues played a key role in the passage of landmark federal legislation that put stringent procedures in place to protect the burial sites and artifacts of all Native Hawaiians and Native Americans. In 1976, the 200th anniversary of the birth of American freedom, Maxwell decided to create a "national incident" to highlight injustices done to Native Hawaiians and assert their land rights by occupying Kaho'olawe Island.

Once an idyllic land opposite Ma'alaea, Kaho'olawe was filled with more than 2,000 cultural sites. Largely uninhabitable because of overgrazing, it was turned into a World War II practice-bombing range shortly after Pearl Harbor. It was still used as late as 1976, and it's still mostly off-limits to everyone, despite a government promise to return it years before.

Tahitians, among the most prominent Polynesians populating these islands eons before, used Kaho'olawe as a reference point to and from Tahiti. (The western portion was called Lae O Kealaikahiki, meaning pointing the way to Tahiti.) The island was regarded as special because it was an ideal departure point for voyages back to Tahiti—the North Star and currents showing the way.

Maxwell handpicked *Kanaka Maoli* from every island for "an invasion." Nine, including Moloka'i activists Walter Ritte Jr. and Dr. Emmett Aluli (my recent colleague on the Maui County Health Care Task Force), made it to shore. Maxwell, who made a preparatory trip the previous fall, plied back and forth in a boat diverting the US Coast Guard while the others landed.

The Kahoʻolawe nine were then eventually captured and arrested, and some served jail time. To make a very long story short, Kahoʻolawe is now a protected preserve, no longer a bombing range. Only partially cleared of unexploded ordnances, it's scheduled to become sovereign Hawaiian territory apart from state or US control.

Maxwell parted ways with the original activists and moved on to other things. Later, the Protect Kahoʻolawe ʻOhana was formed. The group now brings volunteers to the island every full moon to undertake the formidable work of restoration.

Maxwell's priorities over the next three decades were significant: heading the Hawaiian Advisory Committee of the US Civil Rights Commission, chair of the newly created Maui/Lanaʻi Islands Burial Council for many years, and serving as *kupuna* to Haleakala National Park and the Maui County Council.

ACTIVIST REVISITED AGAIN
Charles Maxwell Sr.
Hawaiian Essence Remains with the Bones

IN CASE YOU HAVEN'T NOTICED, Native Hawaiians and Americans are different. According to activist Charlie Kauluwehi Maxwell Sr., American culture is built upon materialism. Hawaiian culture emphasizes spirituality.

Your big responsibility if you live here, the Hawaiian storyteller and cultural practitioner believes, is to understand the place you call home. To Hawaiians, this is a spiritual place and the most basic cultural belief is Hawaiians' respect for the dead.

Unlike Western society, *Kanaka Maoli* believe that part of their essence remains with the na *iwi,* the bones of the dead. And places of *kana* (burials) are sacred grounds.

In 1986, Maxwell got a call from then-Mayor Hannibal Tavares about *iwi* that had been located on the proposed site of the Ritz-Carlton Kapalua on Honokuhua Bay.

The man who was to become head of the Maui/Lana'i Islands Burial Council knew exactly what he had to do.

Construction crews had disturbed 800 graves, among 2,000 or more laid in layers on the site. Landowner Colin Cameron, according to Maxwell, insisted his hotel had to be built on the cliff on the edge of the bay even though the site was filled with gravesites. Hawaiians said, in effect, no way.

Protests began. A vigil was held at Iolani Palace, former home of Hawaiian monarchs. Thirteen hours of negotiations between Hawaiian leaders, Cameron, and then Governor John Waihee took place. Cameron caved—but at a price. He agreed to move his hotel if the state paid $6 million ($10 million in today's dollars) to acquire land for a cultural preserve.

Ever since, Cameron has been variously praised for scrapping his design and relocating the hotel and vilified for fighting the change. Since then, the hotel has partially made amends through its annual Celebration of the Arts cultural festival that fosters a community dialogue with Native Hawaiians.

According to the agreement, Maxwell and six others would be empowered to return 800 skeletal remains to the site, now a grassy field forbidden to walk upon without permission. The *iwi* would be wrapped in *kapa* (also known as *tapa*) especially prepared in the old way. Maxwell describes this on his website: "We started to wrap the remains. We would come...at eight at night and go home at three or

four o'clock in the morning for three-and-a-half months."
On midnight of the last night, as Maxwell tells it, under lit
torches, with a chant about to begin, a Hawaiian exclaimed:
"Eh'ho'ailono" (an auspicious event).

"We came to the edge of the cliff and when we looked
down we barely saw the outline of one *kohola* (whale), turning on its side and slapping the waters."

For 15 minutes, the whale slapped, and the Hawaiians
cried. Owls (*pueo*) flew over, signaling the spirits were re-
united with their *iwi* at Honokuhua. "Whoooo, whoooo,
whoooo, they screamed and went right up to the mountain,"
Maxwell wrote.

"Everyone was dressed in the black *malo* (loin cloths)."
Kahu Charles Maxwell Sr. said he was "privileged to be there."

Hawaiians have an expression, a pledge to ancestors:
La'keha 'O Kou moe lau (the dignity of your long sleep will be
preserved). The Hawaiian soul is in the bones where mana,
their essence resides. Upon death, their mana remained in
their bones. To Kanaka *Maoli,* their sanctity is to be defend-
ed at all costs.

Sensitive issues like lack of respect for the *iwi*, the overthrow of the Hawaiian Kingdom, the concept of land ownership literally foreign to Hawaiians, and the seizing of lands
still embitter many Hawaiians, according to Maxwell.

"About 70 percent of Hawaiians," he says, "know of these
injustices; 60 percent feel resentment and 25 to 30 percent
really are hung up on this and are upset at a quiet majority
that is not involved."

There are at least 20 Hawaiian groups seeking to address
grievances, including those who want the United States to
sanction a Hawaiian nation within a nation and the return
of vast acreages. There are no easy answers. Should the land
serve the culture, the dead, or both? Maxwell is philosophi-

cal, noting that Hawaiians need to move beyond bitterness and can make no progress unless they make the best of it.

Maxwell is here to give such advice, as he proudly points out on his website, after a recent warning from doctors that he wouldn't live six months without slimming down from a very unhealthy 423 pounds. Now, thanks to a crash-exercise program, a healthier Maxwell has lost 173 pounds and has become vigorous again. Yet, the slimming down may have been too late. Maxwell passed away in 2012

KUPUNA
Ke'eaumoku Kapu
Celebrator of the Culture

KE'EAUMOKU KAPU, head of Na 'Aikane o Maui, the increasingly important cultural group, in early life got no respect. Today he is one of the leading practitioners of the culture, honored by leading the Maui group that greeted the Hokule'a voyaging canoe headed around the world. Ke'eaumoku's story is a tale of the struggles faced by many native peoples in modern Hawaii who now are a minority in their ancestral home.

Ke'eaumoku has confronted many of the obstacles placed in the path of his Hawaiian brethren. Yet he has overcome them to bring his culture back to life.

Although he has traced his ancestors back 27 generations to chiefs, he knew virtually nothing of his culture. Now he is an expert, a respected kupuna doing all he can to revive interest in the culture.

During Ke'eaumoku's high school days, suppression of Hawaiian culture was the norm. Taught by his dad, Ke'eaumoku was fluent in Hawaiian. When he used Hawaiian in school, it meant a trip to the principal's office and possible suspension. He liked to challenge authority by speaking Hawaiian.

Keʻeaumoku said he was "brainwashed from the time I was four. If you spoke Hawaiian, it was a sign you were from yesterday. My dad had spent his whole life in Maui but worked in Oahu at a fish cannery. Later, he joined the US Marines and served in Korea," he said.

Born in Oahu, Keʻeamoku described the island as "a concrete jungle. We were living under the State of Hawaii housing system. We didn't have land; we just had an apartment. Hawaiian natives were living at the poverty level.

"Hawaiian wasn't even a required language. No one even knew there was a language. The language survived within the homes of grandfathers and grandmothers," he continued.

"Samoans in school were allowed to speak Samoan, and Filipinos could speak Filipino, but Hawaiian was banned."

When tourists, popularly known today as visitors, began arriving in large numbers, many Hawaiians were not sure it was a good idea. One of these was Keʻeamoku, who like many young Hawaiians at the time thought he got no respect.

His early life illustrates the frustrations of Hawaiians over the last century. Today, on this island, he is perhaps the foremost preserver of things Hawaiian.

Keʻeaumoku, easily today one of the most influential Hawaiians involved with the Lahaina community, is a man of deep convictions. One magical week in 2008, he even walked around the entire island with a group of followers and sympathetic locals just to demonstrate unity with people in Maui's 17 ancient districts. He repeated the long trek again in 2015.

Conviction began to take shape early. At William McKinley High School in Oahu, his task was to raise the state flag each morning. The act was both ironic and distasteful, not because of the flag but who the school was named after.

In 1893, Grover Cleveland, president of the United States, wanted to reverse the US takeover of the Hawaiian Kingdom. He was defeated, however, by William McKinley. McKinley went along with sugar interests, and so Hawaii was officially annexed by the United States in 1898.

The irony of going to a school named after a guy who squashed Hawaiian sovereignty was not lost on Ke'eaumoku.

Neither was the realization that he knew nothing about his own culture.

His own father, John Paul (Hawaiians often took Christian names), would "get whacked" for speaking Hawaiian in class. Suppress the language, the thinking apparently went, and you could suppress a culture—a common goal of some non-natives in those days.

John Paul wanted more for his son, shipping him off to Oregon to get a better education. The experiment had its pluses and minuses. "People made fun and looked at me funny when I spoke broken-up pidgin," he said.

He dropped out at 17, mostly because no one in the family was working then, and he needed to help financially. On returning, his dad joked that "now you sound just like a haole."

At 27, Ke'eaumoku settled on Maui and began growing his own fruit, vegetables, and taro (15 plots) above Launiupoko for subsistence. He also set out to learn as much about the Hawaiian culture as he could, so that his sons and daughters would not be culturally deprived.

In trips to Tahiti and even New Zealand, Ke'eaumoku found elders who could teach him more about Polynesian and Hawaiian culture than almost anyone back home.

Each year, the family makes a cultural pilgrimage to the

island of Hawaii ("'Big Island' is not its Hawaiian name," he said). After the first trip, he got rid of all the furniture in his house except the TV. He told his kids material things didn't matter.

Ke'eaumoku over the years has been involved in multiple groups. He has served on the Maui County Cultural Resources Commission, chaired the Maui/Lana'i Burial Council and Native Hawaiian Historic Preservation Council, and served as a member of the Western Pacific Regional Fishery Management Council. His service of various boards adds up to 30 years.

For several years, Ke'eaumoku was known as the man who wanted to curtail the once raucous Lahaina Halloween celebration as being foreign to Hawaiian tradition. His input spurred the county and the Lahaina Town Action Committee to bring Halloween under better control.

To tap his deep knowledge, the Lahaina Restoraton Foundatin has been working closely with him on its new Imagine project to revitalize the area while respecting Hawaiian values.

Sara Foley, who launched an initiative by the Maui Friends of the Library to transform the Lahaina Public Library front lawn into a Hawaiian garden with Polynesian and native plants, has brought Ke'eaumoku in as member of the group's lawn-planning committee. The effort is newly supported also by the Lahaina Restoration Foundation and a large grant from Maui County,

Ke'eaumoku, his family, and others have agreed to restore an ancient stone wall on part of the lawn and install a new "King's Taro Patch." The family has already planted a test plot and will take care of the new plantings once they are permanently installed.

Supporting the culture is a family affair. Ke'eaumoku's

wife, U'ilani, heads Aha Moku of Hawaii, a group with a museum and education center near the Front Street tennis courts.

Ke'eaumoku would have been a great candidate to sail on the Hokule'a voyaging canoe, the vessel that in 1976 traversed the Pacific to Tahiti to prove how the first Tahitians navigated here. He didn't make the latest voyage in 2016 that has circled the globe to teach Hawaiian values and promote sustainability Instead, the dedicated Hawaiian is busy teaching, protecting, and preserving the culture in Lahaina.

Willie K., top performers, appears at the Maui Arts
& Cultural Center.

FOUR
ENTERTAINERS/ARTISTS

Would you live anywhere else?

—Musician Willie K.

MUSIC EVERYWHERE
Music Makers to Enjoy

"Ooooo oooooo ohoohohoo…" You hear it everywhere from our musicians, the rendition of "Over the Rainbow" (often referred to as "Somewhere over the Rainbow") popularized by Judy Garland and made into practically a Hawaiian anthem by "Iz," Israel Kamakawiwoʻole, a man said to have had the voice of an angel.

Years ago, our family as visitors had the pleasure of hearing Iz, a victim of obesity known as a gentle giant, who has since passed away. We thought he was good, but we had no clue we were seeing a legend in the making.

These days, instrumentalists and vocalists are everywhere—in courtyards, on restaurant *lanai,* and even on the Baldwin Home lawn—and the same people in the know continually show up when one makes a special appearance. Many others, especially visitors and newcomers, often have no clue what they are missing.

Musicians have a rich history, and when they perform, they often tell interesting tales. Here's a kind of guide to top musicians.

Succeeding the drum, *ipu,* and other instruments, the classical guitar appeared in the 1800s, brought by cowboys from Spain and Mexico imported to round up cattle for King Kamehameha III.

More than a century ago, the ukulele made its way to the islands when two Portuguese instrument makers sailed here to work on the sugar plantations.

Soon, even Liliʻuokalani, Queen of the Hawaiian nation and beloved composer of songs still sung today, took the "uke" up and helped popularize it.

A hundred years ago or so, the steel guitar came along,

invented when a bit of metal fell on some guitar strings and produced a unique sound. Electric guitars debuted in the thirties.

But it was the steel guitar that brought us the distinctive Hawaiian music popular in the fifties and beyond; songs like "Little Grass Shack" and "Sweet Leilani" played on 450 radio stations on a program named Hawaii Calls from Waikiki. The show popularized Hawaiian music on the mainland.

Next came the Hawaiian music renaissance, with *hapa haole* (part Hawaiian part Causcasian)songs displaced by ones written and sung in the Hawaiian language.

And then (meaning loosening of keys for slack-key guitar) became so popular that its players have won many Grammys.

Some of the state's best musicians call this place home and others come frequently.

George Kahumoku, a slack-key master and Grammy winner who also keeps busy teaching school and planting taro, started as a child like many of his musical colleagues. He was not allowed to play family instruments, but he would sneak into the woods and strum when his parents weren't paying attention after drinking potent, homemade white lightning. (Venue: Wednesdays at Napili Kai Beach Resort).

Keali'i Reichel, a son of Lahaina, has won 31 Na Hoku Hanohano music awards, including four as Hawaii's top male vocalist and four for best album. This singer, songwriter, and *kumu hula* (whose dancers won at the Merrie Monarch festival) helped pioneer the Hawaiian music renaissance. (Frequent venue: the Maui Arts & Cultural Center).

Amy Hanaiali'i Gilliom began singing soon after she turned one, flourished in Baldwin High School music programs, and has become one of the few contemporary Hawaii musicians to study music in college. This Maui girl—whose great-great-grandmother was a dancer who taught hula to

Hollywood stars for movies with Hawaiian themes—has made 11 albums. She is a big believer in technology, often tweeting off stage.

Willie K., also Lahaina born, wows fans on Maui and the mainland, as well as in Japan, China, Germany, and Israel. When not strumming, he sings opera and mimics a dozen vocalists, including Willie Nelson and Dionne Warwick when he sings "We Are the World." (Venue: Kimo's on many Sunday afternoons)

Richard Hoʻopiʻi, a Grammy-winning falsetto singer who still lives in his native Kahakuloa on the North Shore, is the recipient of the National Endowment for the Arts Folk Heritage Fellowship along with older brother, Sol, his partner in the Hoʻopiʻi Brothers. Richard carries on since his older, legendary brother Sol passed away a few years ago. (Frequent venue: He often plays Hawaiian festivals.)

Henry Kapono, known as the "Wild Hawaiian," is an award-winning singer and composer whose award shelf includes male vocalist of the year, song of the year, and single of the year. (Venue: Dukes in *Honokowai* on the last Friday of the month)

Melveen Leed, Molokaʻi born and a former Miss Molokaʻi, five times named female Hawaiian vocalist of the year, plays on her Yamaha and sings country (Paniolo Country), jazz, and pop music in her fifth decade performing music. She has won numerous Hawaiian music awards for her albums and has been Hawaii vocalist of the year. (Venue: three-hour shows occasionally at KBH)

The power of Iz, who initially played with his Makana Sons of Niʻihau and sold a million copies of his first solo album, goes beyond "the rainbow song." Iz eventually broke away from singing tourist songs and pioneered singing about things Hawaiian. Ironically, his most famous song isn't Hawaiian at all. Iz is gone, but others carry on the tradition of singing in Hawaiian.

LEGENDARY IZ
Israel Kaʻanoʻi Kamakawiwoʻole
Oz and Iz over the Rainbow

THERE WAS OZ, AND THERE WAS IZ. When Judy Garland in The Wizard of Oz sang "Over the Rainbow," it became her signature song for decades. And then came Iz, Israel Kaʻanoʻi Kamakawiwoʻole, gargantuan in size, gigantic in his influence on Hawaiian music.

The Iz version of the rainbow song is now sung just about every day on stage everywhere musicians on Maui gather.

The Iz rendition, heard on a couple dozen TV shows and movies over the years, has become so ever present in Hawaii that some locals continue to believe Iz, wrote it; he did not.

From the fifties into the seventies, when the popular image of Hawaii was hula dancers swaying in glitzy and colorful cellophane, most Hawaiian music was *hapa haole*. Songs like Don Ho's un-Hawaiian "Tiny Bubbles" dominated. Iz was in the forefront of the Hawaiian Renaissance, rejecting hapa haole songs and singing protest and other melodies in the Hawaiian language.

"The story of Iz began May 20, 1959, in the final days of Hawaii's territorial era, three months before the Hawaiian Islands would become America's 50th state. A baby was born in Honolulu's historic Kuakini hospital," wrote Rick Carroll in a wonderful book simply titled Iz.

"Iz was the third child of Evangeline Keale Kamakawiwoʻole, a Hawaiian woman born on Niʻihau, and Henry 'Tiny' Kaleialoha Naniwa Kamakawiwoʻole, a part-Hawaiian born on Oahu. His parents sensed he would be special. They named him Israel Kaʻanoʻi Kamakawiwoʻole. In Hawaiian, his last name translates to "the fearless eye, the bold face."

Iz would spend summers where his mother was born in Niʻihau, Hawaii's eighth island, where more pure-blooded Hawaiians live than anyplace on earth. Iz listened to and played with Niʻihau musicians, who sang songs of old Hawaii in wondrous harmony.

According to Carroll's book published by Bess Press in 2006, Iz had picked up his first ukulele at age six. Already weighing in at 300 pounds as a teenager, Iz made his first professional appearance on a catamaran off of Waikiki. "He then began performing at Steamboats in Waikiki, where his father was a bouncer and his mother was the manager."

When his parents moved to Makaha, he at first refused to go, enamored as he was of the Waikiki scene and the many bakeries he frequented all too often. Iz was already well on his way to becoming morbidly obese.

He would star for 17 years with the Makaha Sons of Niʻihau, a group led by his brother, Skippy, who would die young (28). The last four years of his life, Iz went solo.

One of the Sons' albums, Facing Future, featured Iz singing "Over the Rainbow" and the protest song "Hawaii 78." The album has sold more than a million copies and is the top-selling Hawaiian music album of all time.

The "Hawaii 78" lyrics include the line "cry for the gods, cry for the people, cry for the land that was taken away and then yet, you will find Hawaii."

Ironically, however, the legend of Iz is perpetuated most by his "Over the Rainbow" and its "Oooo" vocals. He had worked to perfect it for months, finally calling a record producer who was still at work at 3:00 a.m. He insisted he record it right away. The album has sold more than a million copies.

The last appearances of Iz on stage before he passed away include June 1997 at our very own Maui Arts & Cultural Center. He passed away 75 days later.

Six years earlier, Iz appeared in Waikiki on NBC's Today show with Katie Couric, and this appearance along with coverage by National Public Radio helped make him famous nationwide.

Still, he was most popular at home. In his final year, Iz blew up to a weight of 750 pounds. His most comfortable place was the buoyancy of a swimming pool.

Jon de Mello, impresario of the Mountain Apple Company that has done so much for Hawaiian music, produced many of Iz's last albums. He described Iz as "a humble man; a person of reality with the ability to relate to all people." He maintains a fan website at iz.com.

How popular was Iz? Hawaii accorded him the rare honor of having him lie in state at the capitol. Some 10,000 people came to his celebration of life on a beachfront.

Iz is now over the rainbow.

SLACK-KEY MASTER
George Kahumoku Jr.
A Grammy-Award Winner Lights a Fire

HE COULD HAVE BEEN A SUCCESSFUL ARTIST or a prolific farmer, or a teacher who could use his skills in art to boost the confidence of troubled high school students, or an itinerant player of music, or a big-name entertainer.

As a matter of fact, for a while, he was all of these, all at the same time. Constantly reinventing himself between struggles to make ends meet, after a bout with cancer at age 27, the energetic and genial Kahumoku, now 60, normally gets only 3 hours of sleep each 24 hours—a good thing, considering his many interests.

Precocious even at four, a keiki who loved to sketch horses on his parents' farm, George won his first scholarship to attend classes at the Honolulu Academy of Art in 1954. More scholarships followed to Kamehameha Schools and then the Rhode Island School of Design (RISD).

He skipped RISD for a full scholarship at the California College of Arts and Crafts in Oakland because it was closer to home. The talented artist, trained as a sculptor, ended up after graduation teaching art to kids in the inner city.

He turned them off putting graffiti on walls and onto to painting giant murals on downtown buildings with permission of an enlightened landowner. City officials were so impressed with this son of Hawaii that they made him art commissioner for California's Alameda County, including Berkeley.

Then opportunity knocked twice. Kamehameha Schools wanted him back in Honolulu to teach art. The job fell through, but he got a reprieve with an offer to start and become principal of a new Kamehameha Schools facility on the island of Hawaii near the legendary City of Refuge.

Struggling to make ends meet, he enthusiastically signed on. Ever restless, however, that, too, yielded still another lifestyle.

Kahumoku started a farm on Hawaii to raise 1,200 pigs a year. This he found was a quick way to go broke, which he did. In 1990, George began playing slack-key guitar at the Mauna Kea Beach Hotel. Management insisted George perform with a partner.

To keep it in the family, he picked his son, Keoki. Hands shaking, playing poorly, Keoki barely made it through the first set, supplementing his poor playing with an even worse voice. No worries.

"At the break," George wrote, "I grabbed Keoki's ukulele, used my wire cutters and clipped each of the strings on his instrument. From a distance, you couldn't see they were not connected."

The two "played" like that for months, musician and pantomime in perfect harmony. (Despite the rough start, Keoki today is a slack-key master and Grammy winner.)

Uncle George (the tag "uncle" is often attached to locals because so many are related to one another) finally figured out the best way to make a living was to play music at the venues along Ka'anapali.

In 1992, George began playing at the Westin Maui, with one memorable, funny result that had nothing to do with music.

While George was living at the hotel, in an ultimate clash of cultures, he and his Hawaiian friends one afternoon decided they had enough of restaurant food. They would revert to their Hawaiian ways, grab a net, and go fishing at Pu'u Keka'a, known to legions of visiting snorkelers as Black Rock.

Bringing along handfuls of peas, like those used by visitors to attract fish, George and friends cast their nets and pulled in a mother lode of *uhu* (parrot fish), *manini* (sturgeon), *aholehole, u'u,* and others.

Figuring they should avoid cleaning their catch at the Westin's spacious pool, they returned to their room, filled up the bathtub with fish for cleaning and flushed the entrails down a single toilet until it clogged up.

The fish would have to be dried. They strung up ropes, lined them with fish, and turned on the air conditioning. Odors of drying fish wafted through the entire floor—the fishermen didn't realize the AC vents circulated air from one room to another.

Time to cook: gather dried keawe wood stacked outside

the Villa Restaurant. Find some rocks around the waterfall. Group the rocks into a small roasting pit on the fourth-floor lanai, and lay a wire shelf from the mini-bar across the rocks. Fire it up—barbecue a huge kala fish on the open fire. Then walk down the beach for a break.

The sirens of fire engines are not often heard along Ka'anapali Parkway, but they were that day. Yellow-coated firemen strung up a long ladder to the room to put out the tiny flames amid the rocks, blasting a big hole in the sliding-glass door with the powerful stream of the firehose. Another day in paradise.

The story is told in A Hawaiian Life, the self-published book George sells at his slack-key performances. Such mischief has been a way of life for a man whose infectious laugh is duplicated only by his wife, Nancy, the sister of his first music publisher.

By the nineties, George was playing 15 to 20 gigs on Maui a week and traveling to the mainland, playing at performing arts centers as far away as Carnegie Hall in New York. Then, with a flash of insight, George adopted a new approach that sent him on the path to winning Grammys.

Why not duplicate on Maui the successful concerts George appeared in on the mainland? He could stage his own weekly concert series and charge admission.

Paul Konwiser, a retired computer whiz with NASA and a big fan, put together the first show. Clifford Nae'ole, the able cultural practitioner at the Ritz-Carlton, Kapalua, offered an auditorium. The Masters of Hawaiian Slack-Key Guitar Concert Series was born.

Years later, George and as many as 20 guest artists a year are still going strong, recently completing well over 300 performances at the Ritz and a new venue, Napili Kai Beach Resort. Dancing Cat Records came calling a few years ago.

Impresario George Winston regarded George's "melodies and his voice as a gentle Hawaiian breeze."

That breeze, plus the slack-key music of a dozen others the last few years, has brought three Grammys and a recent nomination for a possible fourth based on weekly appearances by George and a dozen or more artists, including Uncle Richard Ho'opi'i and up-and-coming Peter de Aquino.

In 2015, George celebrated the 12th year of his slack-key show and told another story. At a very early age in Oahu, he was waxing cars and making $3.00 a day.

He had written a song and played it for come construction workers. They gave him $27.50. He never waxed a car again.

KAHUMOKU REVISITED

George Kahumoku Jr.
Hawaiian and Man of Aloha

STANDING ALONGSIDE HIS FAVORITE GOAT near lush rows of taro. farmer, teacher, award-winning musician, and composer George Kahumoku Jr. reflected on a versatile life. "My music makes the most money, teaching makes the second most money, and the farm always loses all the money," he said. Life to George isn't about money; it's about farming and giving back. All three he has done on Maui after gigs on the island of Hawaii.

He began playing from Ka'anapali to Kapalua where there was more opportunity. Maui's gain, the island of Hawaii's loss.

By the nineties, he was playing 15 to 20 gigs a week and traveling to the mainland, performing as far away as Carnegie Hall in New York. His greatest success was when he started

Masters of Hawaiian Slack-Key Guitar Concert Series where he now plays at Napili Kai Beach Resort.

Recordings of weekly appearances by George and a dozen or more artists, including Uncle Richard Ho'opi'i and up-and-coming Peter de Aquino, have produced four Grammys in a new Hawaiian music awards category. Meanwhile in 1992, with "time on his hands," George joined Lahainaluna High School to teach. He began running an alternative education program for kids on the verge of dropping out. George's approach is motivation through unconventional teaching.

"It wasn't that these kids weren't smart. They just never got direction. There were kids giving birth to kids, or two parents together with six jobs with latchkey kids," he said. High schoolers had to be flunking five of seven courses, have missed two quarters in a row from school, and been absent 44 days to join the program.

George uses art, cooking, and gardening as teaching tools to turn the students on. "How many seeds can you plant in a square foot of garden? How many gallons of water need to flow? It's all math," he explained. Hundreds of kids now lead productive lives thanks to George's interventions.

George also became a "weekend farmer," building a new home on a 4.5-acre plot near Kahakuloa on the North Shore. In Hawaiian tradition, sustainable agriculture is a community way of life. George and scores of volunteers, including residents, his students, and even mainland visitors invited up for the day, have turned four acres of scrub into a cornucopia of agricultural riches.

There are 80 varieties of taro, 3,000 pounds of sweet potatoes in the ground, and 30 varieties of citrus.

A man favoring superlatives, George claims to have 100,000 plants. Much of the output is given away, although taro for poi is sold at modest prices to his Kanaka Maoli brothers and sisters at 10 distribution points around the island.

Back home in Lahaina, munching a succulent papaya from his farm, popping a slack-key album called Drenched in Music in the CD player, a writer struggles to fashion a last good sentence about this amazing man. Finally, it emerges. In essence, George is a Hawaiian and a man of aloha in the best sense of both words.

SINGER-SONGWRITER
Amy Hanaiali'i
"It's All Good"

MOST OF US HAVE A FAVORITE EXPRESSION we use and overuse all the time. For singer-composer Amy Hanaiali'i Gilliom the expression of the month apparently is "it's all good."

It is only a matter of time before the three-time Grammy nominee wins that Grammy. She even says "it's all good" when mentioning her Grammy losses, because she thinks one is coming.

In more ways than one, Amy isn't like most singers of Hawaiian *mele* (songs). Talking story at the Native Hawaiian Chamber of Commerce sometime back, Amy spun a tale offering insights into Hawaiian music, past and present.

The native of Moloka'i is the product of an unlikely meeting in New York City between a talented hula dancer and a steel-guitar player.

As Amy tells it, "everybody in New York was so fascinated (back in the forties) by Hawaiian girls telling some kind of stories with their hands. They didn't know what it was. Back in that day, it was so cool to be Hawaiian.

"Dancing in New York, my grandmother got a very rare blood disease. My grandfather—and he is on the Caucasian side of my family—wanted to meet my grandmother. He played steel guitar and first trumpet for swinging. Sammy Kaye and all the big bands that were coming out at that time," she continued. "Walter Winchell, the famous columnist, wrote a story about my grandmother needing a blood transfusion. So my grandfather said, 'Ah! That is how I will hook up with her.' He went down to the hospital, donated his blood, and two weeks later they were married.

"I don't know what it was about my tutu (grandmother), but she had a thing for steel-guitar players…She married five."

Amy didn't grow up wanting to sing Hawaiian music. "When I was in school in San Diego, I was studying to be an opera singer and maybe go into musical theater. I went to Los Angeles. I auditioned for Les Miserables. My number was 7,392. I finally got in after two days of camping out. I didn't even open my mouth, and they said, 'Next.' So that was it," she said.

"My grandmother, Jennie, was one of the original Royal Hawaiian hula dancers. She had me meet (Lahaina's treasure) Aunty Irmgard Farden, and I found myself learning to sing female falsetto. I had really deep moments with her singing in the old style the kind that makes people cry; the kind that makes kupuna cry. I decided that it's what I wanted to do… so I started writing my own songs and started writing my albums.

"Then I met up with a wonderful person, Willie K., who helped me find my sound. We sat for hours and hours and hours and wrote music. Willie is very Hawaiian but is very much a showman. That is what sets him apart from everybody else; that is what he taught me. Make them laugh, make them cry," Amy recalled.

"When I came home, I knew I wanted to do pop music. Grandmother asked if I could possibly start singing Hawaiian, and I said, 'Well, I will be totally open to it.' I decided to form this umbrella of businesses around me. I've got a really good merchandising manager who takes care of my albums. I have 11 of them.

"I have Hanaiali'i Records, which is my publishing company. As a Hawaiian musician, I try to teach my fellow entertainers that it can't be just about the music. We have to find other ways to merchandise our talent. We have to use social media. We did a concert. We raised $1.6 million for Japan. Life's all good for Amy Gilliom."

PERFORMER
Willie K.
Wondrous Willie K. Revealed

PERHAPS MAUI'S MOST TALENTED, versatile, and popular entertainer as well as onetime Hawaiian Grammy nominee often asks during his performances, "Are there any Willie K. fans out there?" Usually, the crowd goes wild.

Willie K., now past 50, strums at lightning speed and plays on guitar or ukele almost any kind of music (Hawaiian, falsetto, jazz, rock and roll, blues, R&B, Broadway, and now opera).

He has shared stages with Jimmy Buffet, B.B. King, Bonnie Raitt, Mick Fleetwood, Crosby Stills and Nash, and Prince, and he has been nominated for a Hawaiian music Grammy.

He could be equally as famous nationally as the stars he

has played with if he wanted to be.

Willie the last few years has come into his own not only as a musician but as a performer. At eight he played on stage for the first time and was immediately hooked. Asked if he strummed much in high school, he said, "Oh yeah, and in elementary school too."

Willie grew up living in a kind of shack near a mango tree (one of the subjects of the many songs he has written). For years he played for what could be called a pittance. Today, with good paydays, he no longer has to worry about money and chooses to give many performances for free to benefit good causes.

He played at a festival for Women Helping Women. He sponsors an annual Willie K. Charity Golf Tournament, luring in celebrities he knows to play to help cancer victims.

Some 30 years ago, this son of Lahaina went to San Francisco to learn to play rock and roll. "All they wanted me to play there was Hawaiian music," he joked in an all-too-short interview. Learn rock and roll, and much more, he did. With his musical apprenticeship complete, Willie returned to Maui in 1990.

He's been here ever since except for musical forays to perform on the mainland, and in China, Japan, Guam, Tahiti, Israel, Italy, and Germany. He often goes back to Germany.

Maui's luck is that Willie rejected the allure of national stardom to play a number of years at Hapa's in Kihei, the Maui Cultural Center, Mulligan's on the Green, and numerous other venues here.

Rarely appearing in Ka'anapali the last few years—at 14 he played at Sheraton's old Discovery Room and at the former Maui Surf—he now plays regularly at Kimo's and at Hard Rock Café.

Why does Willie live, play, write, and produce music on

Maui? His response is a question: "Would you live anywhere else?"

Today, Willie has a new twist. Although his joy has been to play whatever he wants and play and play and play, he also now talks story during his two-hour show, regaling audiences with funny tales about the early days in Lahaina or experiences on stage.

Willie's personal hero is his father, Manu Kahaiali'i, a crooner and a giant of a man at six foot four who supported many Hawaiian causes and did the Jackson Five with Michael Jackson eight better. Manu had all of his 13 keiki, with Willie the second oldest, perform on stage. The family work ethic—practice, practice—was a daily requirement.

The talented Manu exposed Willie to Waikiki crooner Don Ho and guitar legend George Benson. Willie went on to spend eight months listening to and emulating the many styles of guitar great Joe Cano.

In high school he also mimicked his idol Jimi Hendrix. Eric Guillom, also a fast strummer who partnered with Willie for a while, said playing with him is like playing with Michael Jordan.

His music soars, feet tap, and the laughter during Willie's talk stories would do justice in quantity to a TV laugh track. The wondrous Willie K., a musician's musician, through his talk story, has also become a comedian.

KUMU, COMPOSER, SINGER
Keali'i Reichel
Up and down, up and down

IF HE WERE IN THE SPORTS WORLD, kumu hula Keali'i Reichel would be called a triple-threat man since he excels in three ways. Reichel performs, composes wonderful songs, and teaches hula. He and his *halua* (hula group) have also won two prestigious awards at the annual Merrie Monarch competition on the island of Hawaii.

What it takes to become an accomplished hula dancer is a good question for Reichel, who is as demanding as they come when it comes to learning the techniques. Reichel provided some of the answers during the beginning of his second class. If you are not in the *halau*, you are not supposed to watch.

In this instance Reichel made an exception, granting this observer the rare privilege of attending. Only note taking was allowed and no digital recording.

After two sessions, however, the kumu simply said, "This is the last time you are going to be able to come in. There is a bit of mysticism about hula for it is a bit like a secret society. Only the initiated are supposed to learn its many secrets. Even the new students were required to ask permission before entering the *hale* (gathering place)."

Those passionate about hula say learning takes years of study, daily practice, and knowledge of both the Hawaiian language and the inner meaning of Hawaiian.

To learn the authentic hula of old Hawaii or the modern dances, it has to become an obsession for *haumana* (students), said Reichel, its demanding teacher.

"This class meets only once a week, but for you it has to become an obsession," Reichel noted.

Many of the "new" students had danced hula for years.

All acknowledged it takes a lot of work to learn the authentic hula, absorb the inner meaning of mele and chants, and bring their knowledge to another level.

Learning the language in order to interpret the dances properly is tough. "Keiki absorb the Hawaiian language like a sponge," a student observed. "When you are older, you are still a sponge, but the water drips out."

Over the months, the students fully embraced the kumu's disciplined approach and found, as they learned, that his 30 years of experience teaching hula was already paying dividends.

Let's listen, via scribbled notes (no tape recording allowed), as the kumu instructed his dancers on the beginning "grounding position" at one of the first classes.

"Everything starts from here with flat feet," said Kumu Reichel, pointing to the ground. "Feet flat, toes touching each other, shoulders and body relaxed, arms extended.

"You don't take big steps. You will lose control of your body if you do. Check the position of your feet. Use your extended arm to bring yourself around. You need to control your body from the tips of your toes. That is the name of the game: control.

"Up and down, up and down. Polish this step all week. After five or six weeks, you will be precise. You must practice this, every single day.

"Point your hands with precision. Check the position of your elbows. Bring your hands up to form a flower. When I tell you to freeze, you should have such control over your body that you keep your feet together. I may sound like a broken record, but you have to go all the way down to look nice."

Reichel never did say anything about smiling. But as every visitor knows, a smile and dancing hula go together.

Those smiles extend to the audience. As one visitor noted, you never tire of seeing a beautiful hula.

ARTIST
Jim Kingwell
Painting the Town Red, Green, and Blue

FOR YEARS, FRIDAY NIGHT HAS BEEN ART NIGHT. Every Friday, prolific artist and good soul Jim Kingwell has set up his easel alongside Lahaina sidewalks to lure in crowds.

By his estimate, he has easily painted 3,000 original works of art, many featuring Lahaina Town landmarks.

Though born in Oakland, California, this oil painter and watercolorist has given hundreds of visitors a piece of Maui to take back home—scenes like crowds in front of Cheeseburger in Paradise or ocean view landscapes.

Celebrities like TV sports legend John Madden, Dustin Hoffman, Donald Trump, Olympian Dorothy Hamill, Arnold Schwarzenegger, and art aficionados around the world display his work, often created en plein air (painted outdoors) in Hawaii, Finland, Switzerland, Chile, and even Easter Island.

Kingwell, son of an airline mechanic and grandson of a Finnish masseuse—both his grandparents and father came from Finland—was inspired to paint by a third-grade teacher.

From California, "we started flying to Hawaii on those four-engine prop planes in 1955 when I was five years old," as he tells it.

"We could come on a dime because of the employee discount, and we did that once every other year until I was 14.

"I always had an inclination to draw. I remember drawing on little paper bags in Yosemite," he recalled.

After one Hawaii trip, his teacher asked him to draw on the class chalkboard. "I drew a palm tree, a hula girl, and Diamond Head. It stayed up there for a week. That was a real plus for a kid," he said. This was that moment Kingwell realized he wanted to be an artist.

The would-be artist kept drawing all through grammar school and high school. During high school, "I won a summer scholarship at the San Francisco Art Academy. My folks were ecstatic," he recalled. Later, the college-level program extended a full scholarship. He trained with practicing professional artists. "It was a great school."

Among his teachers was a famous courtroom sketch artist who had drawn the notorious killer Charles Manson in jail.

After six years in the air force and reserves, he turned to painting to make a living, traveling the world. After a failed marriage, he returned in 1989 to Hawaii, "a very healing place," he said.

"I had forgotten how great the weather was, being able to paint outdoors every day."

Working on Oahu, he became friends with Rick Ralston, founder of Crazy Shirts, who suggested Maui was a better place for an artist. Another mentor in the early years in Lahaina was David Paul Johnson, now owner of David Paul's Island Grill.

Kingwell never intended to remarry, but then along came Christine, a vacationer from Seattle, who became the love of his life. Christine got her man. The phone calls between Maui and Seattle just got too expensive, he noted.

After two years under the Banyan Tree, Jim's work went into Lahaina Galleries, Dolphin Galleries, and Sergeant's Fine Art. After 16 years, he now operates his own small gallery nearby.

"I knew diddly about running a gallery," he confessed. Christine became active in the business and got him organized. She also gave him twins, now 12 years old.

"I always try to get one or two days off a weekend, because I don't want to shortchange the family. They are growing up fast," said the doting father.

Kingwell's success is rooted in his ability to create representational art, a romanticized realism that he embellishes with a touch of whimsy.

"I like to capture the initial attraction of a scene that has light or colors I like. A lot of people say my work makes them feel happy. That's good. There's enough negative in the world," he said.

About half of his work is landscapes; the other half what he calls "building art." He has painted hundreds of structures, filling them with colorful characters. The artist has filled hundreds of sketchbooks with drawings of people, many made at airports, which he uses to populate his paintings.

Will the prolific artist ever run out of subjects in Lahaina? "No way," he quickly points out. "There is always something different. Lahaina is changing, too. I almost think I am a historian at time. I paint something that you think is going to be there forever, and it disappears."

Does he have a love affair with Lahaina? I guess so, he smiles. "It's a pretty nice spot."

LANA'I ARTIST
Mike Carroll
Lady Luck Shines, the Carrolls Capitalize

LADY LUCK HAS SHONE BRIGHTLY on highly successful artist Mike Carroll and his wife, Kathy, and both have made the most of it. People said they were "crazy" when they made an offer to buy a falling-down plantation house on Lana'i after just five days on this land. They went on to sell everything in Chicago to begin a new, fruitful life.

Mike and Kathy are friends. On the day Mike exhibited for the first time at the Banyan Tree, we had two things to celebrate. Mike sold two paintings the first day (unheard of). That evening, Mike and Kathy were our very first houseguests in our in new home in Ka'anapali.

Kathy, a public relations specialist, had worked with my wife, Sara, at the American Dietetic Association in Chicago. Mike had been a successful medical illustrator for 22 years after double majoring in art and biology, earning a bachelor's degree with honors in art and attending the prestigious Johns Hopkins University School of Medicine, where he was awarded a master's degree in medical illustration.

Mike had painted as a kid and missed oil painting. Visiting Manele Bay for their 20th wedding anniversary, the couple fell in love with the island, its people, and its rural ways. Two contractors said the rundown house without a roof they wanted to buy should be torn down. The third, according to Mike, said it "had good bones" and took on the project.

The plan was to spend two months in Lana'i to paint and 10 months in Oak Park, Illinois (my hometown).

Back home, on somewhat of a whim, the couple asked a realtor friend how much their home would be worth, and that is when Lady Luck chimed in.

The realtor offered to buy it himself. A second person learned about the house and said she would buy it for cash. The realtor said he would buy it for cash, too, setting up a silent bidding war and a sale without real estate commission, which led the winning realtor to cry all the way to the bank for the winning steep price he paid.

Mike figured he and his wife could live two years without selling a painting. He began painting at the beautiful grounds of the Koele Lodge, now a Four Seasons resort. He gained exposure to well-to-do visitors, who would stand before his easel when he painted on the grounds.

The Carrolls later opened a gallery on a side street and moved from there right onto the town's main square, where they now operate a gorgeous gallery that displays the works of some 20 artists, with Mike's work one of the most popular of the bunch.

Over the years, Mike has been juried into major competitions such as Art Maui and all three statewide Schaefer Portrait Challenges, and he has been painting in plein air competitions on Maui for eight years.

Mike's website (mikecarrollgallery.com) is a showcase for hundreds of his works, which depict everything from rushing streams and picturesque bays to quaint houses, Lana'i and Maui flora, and portraits of wahines, cowboys, and horses at pasture.

"My style is a blend of realism and impressionism," Mike said. "I was trained as a medical illustrator, which is a 'Type A' form of illustration. I moved to Lana'i to loosen my style up a bit. I enjoy painting portraits, still-lifes, landscapes—you name it."

The artist added, "I try to bring out in all of my paintings a feeling of peacefulness...my life in Chicago was hectic enough, and I really cherish the calm I experience on Lana'i."

Everybody on Lanaʻi seems to know Mike and Kathy. When we mention Mike and Kathy to our friends in Lahaina, people often know them as well.

High-energy Kathy—after helping for years with the gallery—has now made her own mark founding and managing the Lanaʻi Family Rescue Center for distressed cats. But that's another story.

POP ARTIST
Davo
From Hippiedom to Warhol

LOOKING LIKE an early seventies-style hippie ("I was a real hippie, not a pseudo one"), hanging out once with Bob Dylan and Joan Baez in Huntington Beach, California, now well dressed and still equipped with long, wavy, blond hair, pop artist Davo has had the kind of life movies are made of. And as a celebrity name-dropper on Maui, he has no superior.

Davo thinks women are the superior beings on the planet and credits (count 'em) about a half dozen of them with all he is or has become.

The special women after his mother include Barbara Pyle, who got him to New York; mentor and founder of the Lahaina Arts Society Alexandra Morrow; and Lynn Shue of Village Galleries, who first displayed his art in a fancy setting.

Davo's life is storybook. Born in Los Angeles in 1950, grew up five miles from Disneyland, and surfed in Southern California.

He gardened for Ansel Adams, the iconic western photographer at Big Sur. "I learned a lot from him."

To avoid the jungles of Vietnam he substituted what he

calls the jungles of Kauai, where he wore next to nothing. Then it was on to Tahiti, where he mostly played and occasionally painted badly, he says.

His idyllic and hippie life lived with all its accompanying habits ended one day when he hurt his back surfing. Needing rehab, he was sent to the New York home of one of the earliest of the influential "Davo women," launching a major life change. There he met pop artist Andy Warhol.

Since he was a kid, Davo reported, "I wanted to be a painter. My mother encouraged me. There were always crayons and watercolors around." After meeting Ansel Adams, he wanted for a time to be a photographer.

By the time he reached New York, he'd gone through Cubist, Gauguinesque, and Daliesque periods. The name-dropping Davo's penchant for friending celebrities got him an invitation to visit Warhol's famous studio, the Factory.

"Andy took a liking to me. Though he was very busy, he let me hang out," Davo said. He observed the artist's pop art technique of beginning with a photograph and turning it into a painting.

The dirt-poor Davo saw the chance to combine both of his interests and actually produce something that would sell.

The choice for his first subject? Sex symbol Marilyn Monroe based on a photo in a newspaper. Warhol's parting words to him when he headed back to the islands were "that would be a great start."

The technique involves making a stencil-like silkscreen of a photograph. A kaleidoscope of paint is daubed on a canvas. Expensive, powerful lights burn the image on the canvas, and embellishments with the brush transform the photo into a work of art.

As Davo tells it, he took his last $100 and had a silkscreen of the Monroe image made by a T-shirt maker. He would use it until it became threadbare.

Back on Maui, with no money to buy expensive lighting equipment, he adopted the nearest best thing: Maui's incredible sunlight. At high noon to this day, he burns images onto canvases with 25-second exposures.

Since 1983, Davo has taken Warhol's method a step further. He mixes phosphorous with acrylic and coats the canvas.

Customers in effect get two pieces of art for the price of one. Turn out the lights, and his paintings glow with a quite different look.

"At first I thought this was gimmicky, but art is anything that moves you. I finally realized there was nothing wrong with that," he said.

On Maui, Davo's uncanny luck continued with a humorous twist. After 10 years at the Banyan Tree art fair, Lynn Shue came up to him under the tree, said she liked his art and way with people, and wanted to bring him into a new gallery.

"Just then she turned around, and a bird made a big dump on one of my paintings. I was thinking, 'I am out of here.'" A lady walked up, loved the painting, thought the "paint" was still fresh and bought it on the spot. She never knew what made it fresh.

The starving artist days are long gone, with his work sold in both the Gallery 505 operated by another key woman in his life, Belinda Leigh, and Village Galleries.

Three weeks after Davo moved to 505, an executive with the Grammy Awards showed up, saw his painting of the Beatles, and said the artist could get tickets to the prestigious awards dinner if he would donate $10,000 worth of art.

Davo figured that would be four paintings. He's been attending for 10 years, has a vote in the competition, and was thrilled recently "to have dinner" with Paul McCartney. The legendary Beatle had a table in front; Davo, in back.

Davo's women have played such a crucial role in his career you'd think most of his paintings would be females. Not so. His favorite subjects have been the Beatles, Rolling Stones, and Einstein, of all people.

"All the women in my life have been so marvelous, and the men can go to hell. But," he added, "not you, Norm."

FIVE
MAKERS OF MODERN MAUI

In 1960, 15 years after the close of World War II, there was no Ka'anapali Beach. There was no Lahaina Luau. There were no catamarans landing on a broad beach. Lahaina was a still a splantation town. Buildings associated with the missionaries needed repair and restoration. The remarkable people of aloha stepped up to do great things.

—The Author

Trilogy Excursions brought the concept of the visitor catamaran to Maui, one of the first innovations to transform Kāʻanapali Beach.

CATAMARAN CLAN
Jim and Randy Coon
Cinnamon Buns and Band of Brothers

THE CINNAMON BUN at one time on Maui reigned as a prime tourist attraction. Read any tourist guide decades ago and you learned of "the famous Coon family" originally from Alaska who led snorkel excursions to Lana'i and served the famous buns on its early morning trips.

Today, the buns are still leaving ovens as new generations of the Coon family continue to serve visitors. Mama Coon baked for the first 10 years, and her daughters-in-law for the next 20. Baking is now farmed out. Early promotional material emphasized the family. Today's ads and brochures tout the Trilogy, seen daily on Ka'anapali Beach with visitors braving splashing waves to climb onboard. Favorite pastime: seeing them get wet.

Offering some of the most popular catamaran trips in the islands, Trilogy Excursions got its start when Eldon Coon and sons Jim and Rand started building a three-hulled trimaran.

Trilogy was picked as the name to describe the three partners. The story of Trilogy's start is fairly well known (there's a book). However, Trilogy's evolution into a company that has sailed hundreds of thousands of people to Lana'i, on snorkel trips to Molokini, and on sunset cruises off Ka'anapali is not.

The storyteller is Jim Coon, CEO, 66, a modest man whose predecessors go way back to 1888! This—in each generation—is an entrepreneurial version of a band of brothers.

The first three brothers established one of the earliest holistic health sanitariums in Washington State. One was also an inventor.

Thirty years later, two of the sons of Meade Coon built a charter fishing boat and sailed for Alaska, operating out of

Ketchikan and Sitka.

Their charter boat catered to the very rich. One day a visitor who happened to own a yacht once owned by gangster Al Capone suggested that a great destination for a charter boat would be Maui and Lana'i. Eldon Coon knew nothing about the pineapple isle. But he would ask everyone he met whether they had been there and what it was like.

Soon he committed to building the Trilogy with Jim and Rand. The Coons had little funds. So as Jim explains, the father and his two sons spent three years building their dream vessel.

"We worked 14 hours a day, 6 days a week, because we just had sweat equity. We started at eight, took an hour for lunch and an hour for dinner, and worked until midnight."

They did just that, and in 1971 they sailed their 50-foot trimaran (three hulls) to Mexico, South America, and even the Galapagos on the way to the South Pacific.

The Trilogy eventually docked in Lahaina. Both Jim and Rand fell in love with paradise as well as a couple of island girls. The first Trilogy excursion to Lana'i launched on July 5, 1973.

Lana'i is privately owned today by computer whiz Larry Ellison. Bill Gates once reserved every airplane that could fly over the island and every hotel room so he could have privacy for his wedding.

Others had tried to start a Lana'i trip but never asked permission. The Coons became the first to ask for an OK, agreeing to restrict tours to weekdays so locals could enjoy their only beach near Lana'i City without having it besieged with tourists. The Coons won landing rights, which they have enjoyed ever since.

Six passengers paying $35 each made the first trip. Jim and Rand captained. Trilogy was on its way to becoming one of the most popular visitor adventures on Maui.

The original Coon family—the third generation is now active in the business—couldn't have imagined six different Trilogy catamarans would bring what easily could be hundreds of thousands of visitors in more than 10,000 annual trips (estimated) to a beautiful snorkeling beach on Lana'i.

While a lot about Trilogy has been the same, change has been no stranger either. Captain Jim and Captain Rand would land on the Lana'i beach and fire up a huge wok.

The captains were the cooks for the midday feast, and today's captains still are. The Coons rarely captain these days but Chris Walsh still does. He's been captaining Trilogy I through Trilogy VI for 33 years.

Trilogy VI now makes the 90-minute run, along with Trilogy I (new ships sometimes take on old names). Frolicking dolphins still frequently greet visitors as they near the Lana'i port but the harbor itself has gotten a major face lift, looking better than Lahaina harbor.

Trilogy added a snorkeling trip to Molokini in the mid-eighties as well as popular sunset cruises from Ka'anapali. The Coon family tradition lives on in Randy's son Riley who is a captain; Denver teaches snuba (a new form of scuba) and works on the boat, and Lilly is in group sales. Jim's daughter, Leanne handles PR and marketing.

Trilogy paved the way for visitor catamaran sailing on Maui, with a half dozen other companies scrambling for visitor dollars.

One thing never changes: the cinnamon buns.

LUAU PIONEERS
Michael Moore
Bringing Hula to Thousands

CHANCES ARE GOOD that when a visitor asks a local about the best luau the answer will come back, "Old Lahaina Luau." Though all others are enjoyable and fun, Old Lahaina to many stands in a class by itself in quality and contributions to the community.

Talk with lead partner Michael Moore, and it is quickly apparent that this culturally significant, enormously popular enterprise represents perhaps this side's most successful homegrown business since Maui became a magnet for tourists.

Fortune magazine each year lists the most admired and best companies to work for. It is no exaggeration to say that the company named Hoaloha Na Eha (meaning four friends) might just make one of the lists.

The luau's long journey began more than 25 years ago when Oregon-born Michael Moore and accountant Robert Aguilar were working for the Ocean Activity Center. Management of the 505 Front Street center suggested the tourist company start a luau.

Moore, then a sales representative, was intrigued, thinking it would be nice to be an evening bartender there. Moore was used to steering visitors to luaus. "I told people luaus were kind of corny; the food is not that great, but you are in Hawaii so do it."

Three months after the luau opened, the Ocean Activity Center backed out, thinking the luau "did not have much potential." Moore, Aguiar, Kevin Butler, and Tim Moore thought otherwise.

They raised funds and birthed what has become the most

authentic luau in the islands. Not everyone was impressed. In the early years after its founding along the shoreline at 505 Front Street, a Honolulu critic called it the worst luau in the islands.

In typical Oahu-is-the-center-of-the-universe fashion, the critic claimed the best one was at the Royal Hawaiian Hotel. He said that the luau on Oahu was best because you could sip a great cabernet with a view of Diamond Head—a measuring stick of dubious merit, Moore noted.

"At first, the review pretty much devastated us. We really loved what we were doing, and it was a lot of fun. After a few days of being distressed, we said, 'Let's take this review as a template for change to the luau.'

"We added flower leis, upgraded all the food—we really looked at every aspect of what we did, including the way we greeted people. We made it more Hawaiian and personal," Moore said.

"We felt there was a need to present Hawaiian music in a really respectful way that honored the culture—that didn't make fun of it. People were making fun of poi, a staple of the Hawaiian diet, and you can't."

What Hoaloha Na Eha did over the years, as Moore puts it, was "raise the bar of what a luau could be. These were mostly hotel functions. We visited every commercial luau in the state. We wanted to create something that honored the culture. We did that very well for 12 years at 505 Front Street," he continued.

"And then we wanted to build an outdoor culture theater. Hoaloha Na Eha added a new venue oceanside from Lahaina Cannery Mall. The spacious grounds provided for a place for culture demonstrations before the feast and hula show."

Hoaloha Na Eha was also lucky to acquire a kitchen at an adjoining pizza restaurant that had closed. There it could prepare luau meals featuring Hawaiian and American fare. The company also opened Aloha Mixed Plate, which quickly became a popular gathering spot for locals. Today, Hoaloha Na Eha owns and operates the Old Lahaina Luau, Feast at Lele, Aloha Mixed Plate, Star Noodle, Leoda's, and a growing catering business.

The company built a new commercial kitchen and 3,000-foot warehouse *mauka* of Honoapi'ilani Highway, preferring to build there rather than clutter up the oceanfront.

Old Lahaina's claim to fame is authenticity. You'll find no fire dancing there. That's a Polynesian custom. Hawaiians never danced with fire, according to Moore.

Ten years ago, according to its website (www.oldlahainaluau.com), Old Lahaina Luau had boosted annual sales from $600,000 in its early years to $10 million today. Michael is a bit embarrassed by the number that was online. When asked how much the Hoaloha Na Eha enterprises now take in, he just smiled.

The luau "that didn't have much potential," Old Lahaina Luau now welcomes 400 guests a night, 7 days a week during peak tourist times. That's close to an amazing 10,000 guests a month. That's a lot of poi and a lot of hula.

GALLERY OWNER
Jim Killett
An Artful Journey

AS THE ART CAPITAL of the Pacific, Lahaina boasts more galleries per capita than almost anywhere. Had it not been for a lot of rain in Germany back in the seventies, things might have been different for Jim Killett, former small-college football player, football coach in Okinawa of all places, and ex-marine.

He and his wife, Nancy, once a gymnastics coach, wanted to travel the world. Killett, a self-admitted conservative sort who started saving for retirement right out of school, decided to take a risk and pour all of their life's savings into a business.

"It took guts to quit my job," he said. It rained a lot in Germany and Killett took to watching a lot of TV, especially the hit show Hawaii Five-0. Killett fell in love with Hawaii and, knowing he could move anywhere, chose Maui.

Landing in Wailuku in 1976 with no job, he stopped by a real estate agent who was advertising for a salesman but found by a twist of fate he was out to lunch. Killett then drove to Lahaina, saw the harbor, and knew he did not want to live anywhere else.

An ice cream parlor and an art gallery were for sale, but the ice cream shop was taken off the market. So Jim ended up calling Nancy back in Arkansas to proclaim, "We just bought an art gallery."

Jim knew nothing about art. "Lahaina Galleries had one painting for sale by David Lee; it sold art prints and even puka shells." In the early days, Jim used to ride his bicycle along Front Street with the gallery open but no customers. When a customer entered, he'd hop off the bike.

More than four decades later, Lahaina Galleries is one of the most successful businesses of its kind in the state with galleries in Lahaina and Wailea, and on the island of Hawaii.

Lahaina Galleries today represents 21 international artists, many who live here. Three were born in Italy, another in Brazil. And still another began in France and settle din Lahaina. And still another hailed from Argentina.

How did the former football and gymnastics teacher do it? Apparently with a lot of luck, good ideas, and honest operating methods (some art dealers have been known for their crass selling methods). He did very well.

Starting with the talented David Lee in 1970, the Killetts signed on two other budding stars, Paris-born Guy Buffet, known for the whimsical Parade of Cows, scenes of old Hawaii and Paris bistros, and marine artist Robert Lynn Nelson. Lahaina Galleries was one of the earliest promoters of marine art, nurturing Nelson's career until he moved on with Jim's blessing to establish his own gallery.

Buffet is still with Killett after all these years. Lahaina Galleries has spawned many imitators, propelling Lahaina Town from a place with only 2 or 3 places selling art to more than 21 galleries today. Another key move, initiated by Jim and the Lahaina Town Action Committee's Joan McKelvey was the start of Friday Night Is Art Night, in which galleries host some of their artists and offer visitors snacks and wine.

Lahaina Galleries' artists make up a true *'ohana*, dropping in on art night even when they are not scheduled to appear. On a recent Wednesday Art Night in Wailea, artists known as the Twins could be found explaining how the gilt frames they make enhance their Renaissance-style paintings the two collaborated on to paint. In front of a handsome bronze Hawaiian figure, sculptor Dale Zarella explains his technique.

Serigraphs start at $500. The most expensive art: $500,000 fashioned by the late renowned sculptor Frederick Hart.

These have been largely sunny days for the Killetts on Maui. The Killetts' flagship Front Street gallery in Lahaina recently closed but an alliance with another gallery is in the works. Those rainy days in Germany, however, are long past. There are no more puka shells in the gallery, and Lahaina averages only 12 inches of rain a year.

COMPOSERS, SINGING, DANCERS
Farden family
Sweet Voices, Sweet Musicians, Sweet Hula

IN THE LATE 1890s a friend of the man who would become a patriarch of musicians and dancers told a young student, "Charlie, your voice is a gift from God," author Mary Richards reported. "When you marry, you must have lots of children, and you must all sing."

In Annie Shaw of Ka'anapali, Charles found someone with an equally golden voice. The sweet voices of Charles Keka'a Farden and Annie Shaw were brought together in marriage in 1897 and they eventually had 13 children.

This fabulous Farden family became a legend in music and dance, their songs and dances still alive today.

Irmgard Farden Aluli, one of 13 children, secured a college degree in home economics, taught school, bore and mothered 11 of her own and penned more than 300 songs in praise of the islands.

The talented composer wrote the song "Puamana," still popular today, about the place where high chiefs once lived and the site of the family home not far from the present Lahaina Shores.

Nane Aluli, Irmgard's son, who ran the Mauian Hotel in Napili, remembers his mom writing lyrics on napkins when words came to her during lunch or other spare moments. Irmgard's sister, Auntie Emma Farden Sharpe, won renown as one of Lahaina's greatest na kumu hula.

Charles, once played football before Queen Lili'uokalani at prestigious Punahou School, married Annie on the day she graduated from a missionary school in Makawao.

Charles had landed a job at Paia Sugar Mill, and before long the young couple was off to Lahaina. Farden was chosen to be one of the *luna* (bosses) at the brand-new Pioneer Mill. Soon, little Fardens began to sing in cane fields, at family gatherings, and on stage.

The most passionate dancer of hula was, who at 15 dreamed of taking lessons from the renowned Kauhui Likau, a Royal Court dancer for kings and who had been trained since infancy. Emma prayed and prayed, the book Sweet Voices of Lahaina recounts, and a reluctant kumu hula was finally won over by the young girl's pledge to pass on the ancient hula techniques to new generations. And that she did.

Some of Emma's charges are still dancing hula at resorts today. Until she passed away, Emma never stopped performing with a troupe that danced everywhere from the Maui Palms in Kahului to the Sheraton in Ka'anapali. In the eighties, thousands rode the elevator to the top of the Sheraton Hotel to enjoy authentic Emma hula.

Others family members distinguished by their voices and the number of instruments they played—almost always including ukulele—were Annie, soprano, two instruments; Maude, soprano, three; Edna, soprano, three; Diana, soprano, two; Bernard, baritone, four; Carl, tenor, six; Buddy, baritone, four; and Rudolph, tenor, three.

When Charles Farden was told in his teen years he must have many children to sing together, no one—least of all Charles—probably ever imaged how well his friend's prediction would come true. Not the least of which, they would all play instruments, too.

KUMU HULA LEGEND
Emma Sharpe
A Legend Celebrated

DELVING INTO THE HISTORY of Lahaina's fabulous Farden family and beloved kumu hula Emma Farden Sharpe is a bit of a challenge since there is so much untold. For new generations, Sharpe may be just a name.

But lively, redheaded Emma Sharpe may have been among the most influential and important figures in Lahaina post-monarchy history.

The topic is well worth pursuing further. From the twenties through the late eighties, this fabulous Farden, as she was known, dominated entertainment in the Hawaiian style. She brought authentic hula to uncounted thousands of visitors.

More important, according to nephew Hailama Farden, now a vice principal of Kamehameha School in Oahu, Emma learned the traditional hula she passed on to thousands from two dancers. One was her first teacher, a young girl, Kauhai Likua, a dancer from Kamehameha IV's royal court.

Another was Oahu kumu Joseph Ilala'ole. Some 90 percent of hula taught today can be linked to the styles of Auntie Emma and this second teacher.

Emma taught primary grades at Kamehameha III Elementary next to the harbor on Front Street starting in 1923. The most significant lessons she gave were in hula. She taught and helped preserve the dances of antiquity to dancers who themselves would become leading na kumu.

These dancers included the legendary Nina Maxwell and grandniece Kathy Holo'aumoku Ralar. All brought these traditions to newer generations of dancers.

Special insights into the Farden legacy were presented one weekend in a performance at the Maui Arts & Cultural Center where the Farden-related *'ohana* performed and at Holy Innocents Church near the 505 Front Street shopping complex Sunday where Hailama Farden of today's generation was present as two new feathered *t* (royal standards) were unveiled.

The *kahili* were created with financial support from none other than Edna Pualani Farden Bekeart, the last of Emma's seven sisters to survive. Emma herself made it to only 87, still performing while in her mid eighties.

One of the many highlights of the cultural center performance was the singing of the classic Hawaiian melody also called "Puamana," composed by Emma's prolific songwriting sister Irmgard Farden Aluli. Irmgard's father, Charles, composed the words, and Auntie Irmgard composed the music in 1937.

A revealing line says a lot about what the illustrious family was all about. It talks of the Puamana homestead as "a place of happiness, where there was a lot of family love."

The song also describes Puamana's swaying coconut trees. With each birth, the family planted a coconut tree to symbolize each child's growth. Each tree rose tall except one, which grew horizontally and at first produced poor fruit. The baby that tree was planted for never made it into adulthood.

Family members' appreciation for each other is shown in a YouTube video, with Emma dancing and Irmgard playing uke and singing. "This is my sister, Emma," Irmgard says with a great deal of pride. A video of Auntie Emma can be seen by going to YouTube and searching for Emma Kapiolani Farden Sharpe. More than 14,000 people have watched it.

Nearly 100,000 people have viewed a video of the song "Puamana," performed by *na halau* throughout the world. The popularity of hula overseas can be ascribed in part to Emma, who not only traveled to Oahu to teach but also to places like Spain and Japan.

Kaʻanapali, however, was one of the places Emma really soared. The 18 dancers of the Puamana troupe led by Emma danced nightly for years in the sixties at the new Sheraton, the former Maui Surf where the Westin is now, and other places.

Kaʻanapali Beach Concierge Malihini Heath, a good friend who performed with Emma and was with her when she passed away, remembers frantically running up the hill below the old Discovery Room to make the show on evenings when the group danced at more than one hotel.

Kanoelani Aquino, another student who danced for more than 15 years in Kaʻanapali, took lessons for five years when Emma lived in Kahana. Emma gave her the Hawaiian name Kanoelani, which means heavenly mist, because of the joy the future Mrs. Rudy Aquino exhibited when it was about to rain. Kanoelani, who was in charge of watering Emma's lawn, would jump for joy since a good rain meant she would not have to water.

Every two years Emma would hold an often-spectacular *uniki,* a traditional-hula-class graduation ceremony usually attended by hundreds. Dancers who learned from Aunty later could be immediately identified as her students by the distinctive way they performed.

Emma's style has been described as "flowery," Fingers flow (and) are together. They flow very, very gracefully, not so regimental and straight."

Graceful, smooth, and joyous, Emma Sharpe demonstrated her passion for hula at every show. She was also a person "nicer than nice," her nephew said.

HISTORY BUFF
Jim Luckey
Luckey for Lahaina

LIKE THOUSANDS of other visitors before and since, Oregon sawmill salesmen Jim Luckey fell in love with Maui on his very first visit and thought he would like to live here.

Luckey and his wife, Annie, wasted no time, moving to Lahaina a couple of years later to start a new career. Luckey for Lahaina.

Competing with 23 other candidates, Luckey succeeded Larry Windley to become the third director of the pioneering Lahaina Restoration Foundation in 1973.

For the next 26 years, Luckey spearheaded the preservation and restorations of irreplaceable sites, including the seamen's cemetery alongside Maria Lanakila Church, the steep-walled Old Lahaina Prison, the Seamen's Hospital, and the Wo Ho Temple (a meeting hall built by Chinese immigrants), and other projects.

His pride and joy was the printing house. When the restoration began birds were roosting in the 125-year-old rafters, there was a hole in the roof, and the place was falling apart.

The printing house was built with stone carried high up the hill to Lahainaluna Seminary by students. The restoration team replaced 23 sets of decaying window frames, fixed the interior, and added a new shingle roof with the same number of rows of red shakes building had when it was new.

The industrial arts department of MCC built a 600-pound working replica of the original press used to print grammars and Bibles in Hawaiian, and Luckey had it carried by brute strength into the refurbished structure. Artifacts and displays were added before the opening in 1981.

The Seamen's Hospital became the office of architect Uwe

Schultz who played a key role in its restoration Later Paradise TV, the visitor channel, moved in, paying an annual rent and filling TV screens with Lahaina history.

Luckey put Lahaina in the forefront of a national restoration movement, roving the eastern US historical sites for ideas and pioneering the concept of adaptive use. He knew that not every building could be turned into a museum.

Adaptive use became a buzzword in the preservation movement in Washington, DC. You cannot restore everything and make it a museum. "I like to think that Lahaina was on the forefront of this movement."

Under the leadership of Keoki Freeland and Theo Morrison, executive directors who succeeded Luckey, the landmark Pioneer Mill smokestack was saved and then restored. Luckey was named, executive director emeritus, and took a well-deserved retirement.

He at kast would be able to fish.   No, I didn't do much fishing while in Lahaina," he said, Jim passed away in 2015.

MILL MANAGER
Keoki Freeland
Fighting the Good Fight for Lahaina

LAHAINA-BORN, DEBONAIR in his broad-brimmed hat bedecked with a feather lei, three-eighths Hawaiian, an engineer by training, Keoki Freeland retired from Pioneer Mill and then fell in love with town history. In a new career as executive director of the Lahaina Restoration Foundation Keoki has done all he can to preserve the town. As he tells it, Lahaina Town as we known it may have been approaching its deathbed.

In 1962, Lahaina was still a plantation town. Newly built

Ka'anapali Beach Resort was pushing real estate values in town to unheard-of levels. A few town "fathers" wanted to tear down all of Lahaina and build a new Waikiki. Amfac, one of the biggest landowners and most enlightened bene-factor, said no. Lahaina, the company believed, should be preserved as a historic town, as a magnet for tourists in need of more than a beach.

One large property owner in Lahaina was ready to sell out. But another said no. And up stepped Amfac, cosigning a note that allowed the second landowner to buy out the first, preserving Lahaina for future generations.

Soon after, people like Oregon businessman Jim Luck-ey, aided by an all-Amfac board of directors, formed the LRF. Two separate historical preservation districts were soon formed.

The Baldwin missionary home on Front Street was re-stored so effectively that the powerful Baldwin family—still its owners—gifted the home to the foundation along with surrounding lands that are now home to the Lahaina Public Library, an art gallery, and parking lots. All contribute rental income that helps finance foundation efforts to this day.

But the fight for Lahaina was not over, as we shall soon see. Keoki Freeland is in the thick of the effort to maintain, restore, and interpret Lahaina.

Keoki's grandfather, a transplant who moved from Can-ada, built the Pioneer Inn, operated it until 1925, and fa-thered seven children with his full-blooded Hawaiian wife. Keoki's dad became a movie impresario, operating six movie theaters—one at Pioneer, and five on nearby plantations (a new feature every night, Filipino on Mondays, Japanese on Thursdays).

Keoki worked in the pineapple fields to get in shape for athletics at Lahainaluna High School. "We tried to load those trucks fast so we could sit down and rest. But they would just send in more and more trucks! So we would load those buggers up."

Then it was off to college at Notre Dame, separate degrees in mechanical and industrial engineering. "I liked to be around machinery," he explained, and a 33-year career in the sugar industry ensued. This included 21 years at Oahu Sugar and 10 years at Lahaina's Pioneer Mill.

"When I started," he noted, "there were 27 plantations and 11,000 acres in sugar." Over time, Freeland designed machinery, became superintendent of field operations, and then first superintendent of both field operations and the mill, the number-two position in Lahaina.

Along the way he married a native from Kohala, Hawaii Valley, who was a descendant of Hawaiian royalty. It wasn't long before she took to putting paint to their drab plantation-house walls. Thus began Betty Hay Freeland's long career as well-known impressionist artist.

With sugar on the way out, Keoki retired from the mill in 1995 only to see it close four years later. Before he left, he was instrumental in developing for Ka'anapali what he said was the world's first scientifically developed coffee, an effort only now paying off.

Recruited by the LRF, Keoki asked why they wanted an engineer. "I thought these guys were nuts. I had no idea of town history, but I found it very interesting."

Under the 25-year stewardship of Jim Luckey, executive director emeritus and honorary director, and now Keoki, the foundation has flourished. It now manages nine historic sites and has five museums, including the Old Lahaina Courthouse and Hale Pa'i, site of the printing museum.

The foundation preserved the landmark Pioneer Mill smokestack and commemorate their loved ones and businesses in a circle of printed bricks around the base.

Amazingly in August 2010, the company that built the original smokestack more than a century ago is still around, It used old plans to restore a gleaming new white top against a brilliant blue sky to complete its restoration. Lahaina's principle landmark as seen entering the harbor again stands proud.

VISIONARY
Theo Morrison
She Jumps off Cliffs

YOU COULDN'T KEEP her down on the farm. Theo Morrison, a self-proclaimed "cliff jumper" doing her special thing again after leaving community service to raise hens, returned and to bring fresh ideas and her can-do spirit to the Lahaina Restoration Foundation, Her newest commitment is promoting and preserving the history of Lahaina and enhancing the small town she loves.

Sailing from the West Coast, this onetime resident of tiny Ojai, California, arrived on the island of Hawaii with two kids, an art degree, and $1,000 in 1979. She rented a storefront for $200 a month and built a successful business (employing six people) designing and selling artistic baskets. Then the market collapsed due to Philippine imports.

Moving to Lahaina, she soon was volunteering as president of the Lahaina Arts Society. Not long after, in 1991, she pestered the fledgling Lahaina Town Action Committee (LAC) to give her a job running the group that had created Friday Night Is Art Night and an organized Halloween celebration.

Recalling that when she started, "I didn't know what I was doing." Theo found in herself a talent for learning along the way and getting things done. She had the all-too-rare knack for recognizing a good idea and relentlessly and passionately pursuing a goal by getting talented people to help.

During 14 years at LAC, Theo and a team of loyal volunteers managed or created 11 community events, including A Taste of Lahaina, The Best of Island Music, Maui Chefs Present, and the prestigious International Festival of Canoes.

By 2005 she passed the torch to others and left LAC for a new challenge: agriculture. Knowing nothing about farming, she nevertheless now successfully mothers more than 200 hens reared from mail-order chicks.

Twelve dozen eggs a day, plus , beets, and carrots from her "Neighborhood Farm" are sold to Pacific'O Restaurant and several dozen neighbors. For added income (while still farming), in 2006 she joined Lahaina Bypass Now dedicated to building an alternate route above Lahaina to relieve traffic congestion.

Putting the organization on the map, she organized a transportation workshop that helped the Department of Transportation design future projects, installed bike racks throughout town, and pushed for and was successful in getting a new Lahaina bus route for local commuters.

When an opportunity to succeed Keoki Freeland at the LRF opened up, she couldn't resist. As the new executive director, she already has instituted candlelight night tours of the Baldwin Home and organized Bath Day to scrub Lahaina sidewalks. She also started a Hawaiian music festival and held two progressive dinners at historical sites to raise money for scholarships.

What makes a community treasure like Theo—who rarely ever says no—Theo? Vision, passion, tenacity, and leadership.

To organize the first Taste of Lahaina, Theo and Kathleen Leonard, a friend, went to the newly opened Lahaina Center and boldly asked for $10,000 and the use of its parking lot. The center wanted a budget.

"We had none," Theo reported. Before Kathy could speak, she kicked her on her leg under the table. "No problem," Theo chimed in. The next day, they had their budget, and the event later went well.

Then Jerry Kunitomo of B.J.'s Chicago Pizzeria (now Lahaina Pizza) came along and pressed the Lahainatown Action Committee to include music. Over the years, the event got bigger and bigger, achieving a peak attendance of more than 20,000.

The canoe festival was born when Theo, Michael Moore of Old Lahaina Luau, and Kunitomo wanted to stage a cultural event. "Canoes were important. Hawaii would not have been populated without them," Theo noted.

She wrote a grant for a street festival, and the canoe fest was on its way. The next year, Theo recounted, cultural practitioner Kimokeo Kapahulehua came along and announced at a meeting at Gerard's Restaurant: "OK, this year we will cut down trees, get carvers, and make canoes," he said.

"Virtually everyone was stunned," Theo remembered. Kimo got beautiful logs from Kauai, and hotels were lined up to sponsor canoes. By the third year, the festival expanded to include a parade, launch ceremony, and music.

"Presented with an idea like this, people will not just jump off a cliff and do it," Theo said. "I am a cliff jumper. You don't need to know how you are going to get there. I am passionate about getting things done. It is so cool to come up with an idea, get a bunch of people together, and make it happen. It wasn't just me. It was teams of people doing what it took. I think it's fun. I don't consider it work."

In essence, that's been her winning formula for success every time. Her strategies have been based on strong philosophies. Lahaina thrives by bringing people in to events that showcase its heritage, preserve its history, and enhance the streetscape. She has a certification from the National Trust for Historic Preservation in Washington, DC, as a main-street manager.

Theo has a philosophy about farming, too. "We need to demonstrate that sustainability is important and works. In the forties, we were self-sufficient here. This is the way it should be. Kids now think if it doesn't come in a package, you can't eat it."

Without Theo, Lahaina wouldn't be what it has become today. At college in San Francisco, later living in the country, and then in a small town, she figured down deep she was really a small-town girl. Lucky for Lahaina, this is where she put down her roots.

ARCHITECT
Uwe Schulz
Unsung Lahaina Hero

WHEN UWE SCHULZ, chief onsite architect of a boutique shopping center that came to be called Whalers Village, landed in California on vacation in 1970, he spoke barely a word of English.

Architect David Carlson Beale, a developer of strip malls, wanted to turn a large swath of land at the new Kaʻanapali Beach Resort into a European-style shopping center. He looked for a European-trained architect to help.

Uwe (pronounced Uve in Hawaiian) filled the bill perfectly. Within two weeks of being hired, he was onsite. And he has stayed for the last half century, watching over its design as Whalers Village changed over the years and beginning decades-long service to Lahaina.

He has helped with restoration of the Baldwin Home, orchestrated the restoration of Hale Pa'i (the "House of Printing" at Lahainaluna High School that produced Maui's first Bibles and grammars in Hawaiian), and been involved in almost every historic building restoration since.

Retelling a funny story on how he happened to land the job in Palos Verdes, California, Schulz told how Beale had gone home to his wife, who was cooking at the time.

"I had the strangest thing happen today. I interviewed this guy who was born in Germany. I couldn't understand what he telling me," Uwe quoted Beale as saying.

"Barbara Beale was a total nut for Mercedes," Uwe explained. "If she drove, it had to be a Mercedes."

She turned around and said, "The Germans built the Mercedes, didn't they?" David apparently bought the argument.

"And that," Uwe said, "is how I got hired."

In the sixties, Uwe observed, the entire stretch of land from what he calls the Hilton (now Maui Ka'anapali Villas) along today's beach walk all the way to the Hyatt Regency Maui was empty—useless land unsuitable for growing cane or anything else.

Owner Amfac (then Amfac/JMB Hawaii LLC), operator of Pioneer Mill, offered sugar workers in the forties parcels for $2,000 each to build homes. There were no takers. Today the plots are worth millions.

Though a strip-mall builder, Beale wanted to build a center that would create shopping in a museum-like setting to celebrate whalers and whaling. And that's what it became—a showplace of low-rise shops, a signature 30-foot skeleton of a whale at the entrance, a whaling boat near the center, and a first-floor museum complete with whaling artifacts.

The Beales are gone now. The museum is tucked in an upstairs corner, recently stripped of a place to view whaling videos. New owners have also filled the center with freestanding merchant kiosks, some obstructing views of the ocean.

Despite these sad changes, Uwe's overall site design and ambiance remains.

Uwe's biggest contribution, however, may be the preservation of historic Lahaina.

"I came here 40 years ago and saw all these (historic buildings) falling apart," he commented.

The Lahaina Restoration Foundation retained Uwe to help save them. One of his most amazing contributions was the challenge of the old Seamen's Hospital up Front Street past the historic district.

One day, sitting in the office of Executive Director Jim Luckey, he told of overhearing a phone conversation Jim was having with a contractor to haul away the remains of the Seamen's Hospital for $2,000.

"It was just rubble. It was a safety hazard for kids, and there was no money to save it." Uwe came to the rescue.

The increasingly prosperous architect decided to take out a $300,000 personal loan from Bank of Hawaii and restore it himself, after the site was acquired from the Bishop Museum.

"I put my fortune on the line. The interest back then was 16 percent, but I paid the loan back," Uwe explained.

Noted Harold Hyman, a fellow Rotarian who sat in on an afternoon interview, "You're kidding!"

Uwe went on to explain that he took out a 20-year lease from the foundation, which had acquired the site. He moved in his architectural office with six staff members.

It took 10 years before he found another tenant, Jim Kartes of the Paradise TV, who loved it. Rent from Kartes helped pay back a portion, but not all, of the loan. Uwe repaid the rest and turned the Seamen's Hospital over to the foundation.

The hospital had been built by King Kamehameha III, one of Hawaii's greatest and longest-lasting monarchs, as a personal retreat. The structure was constructed from unbelievably strong cut coral as keystones on four corners affixed with fieldstone forming the walls. Old stone, and some new from nearby fields, completed the restoration.

Uwe over the years has also helped restore the Wo Hing Museum, which also had been falling to decay. And when not busy with restoration, he was doing his day job, designing numerous homes ("starkly modern; not appropriate in Hawaii"). He later signed on as an advisor for the renovation of Lahaina Public Library.

Even with all this activity, Uwe never talked much about his other life. Few who knew him from his Rotary were aware of his other enthusiasms.

One was travel. He made two joclub urneys to Egypt, one of the cradles of good architecture, and went to Peru, Japan, and China, where he sought to learn Asian concepts of buildings that he could bring to Maui.

The last year of his life, after being diagnosed with cancer Uwe made his last stand. The sign on the door in the J-Building condominium high above Whalers Village said simply, "Caution: Oxygen in Use."

Inside, family and friends, including first wife Pam and a hospice worker to help, sat alongside the architect who played a central role in restoring historic Lahaina. In bed in the living room, he made his last stand.

Before the end, in an act of bravado, the strong-willed Uwe rose from a bed at Maui Memorial Medical Center, got on three planes—from Maui to Los Angeles to Munich, Germany, to Nairobi, Kenya—and went on a three-week safari over rough roads and muddy terrain.

Fellow Rotarian Harold Hyman called the trek to Uwe's fourth continent nothing short of amazing. Uwe delighted in seeing elephants in the wild despite the challenge of failing eyesight and regaled his companions with stories of trips almost everywhere in Europe to the Great Wall of China, as well as to Australian and New Zealand reefs.

Mention anyplace, Harold said, and it would always be, "I scuba-dived there." And then there was sailing his own vessel in the race from Vancouver to Maui and road racing someplace lost in the columnist's notes.

Uwe returned to the hospital after his African trip. He later made a luncheon visit in a wheelchair to the Rotary club that he had belonged to for 40 some years (he is a Paul Harris Fellow for his donations many times over).

Uwe was a quiet sort of man, never boastful of his many achievements. Among his last was helping Rotary and the Maui Friends of the Library in plans to modernize the Lahaina Public Library.

For whatever reason, friends say, Uwe had never gotten a lot of recognition. He was touched when my "Voices of Maui" column on him ran last year; Uwe has the clipping posted in his office along with a proclamation of praise from Mayor Alan Arakawa. The author was touched, too, when Uwe said, "it was my best Christmas present." Uwe passed away in 2015.

CHEF
Peter Merriman
Pied Piper Pampers Patrons

CHANCES ARE if you dine at many of our Maui's fine restaurants you will enjoy Pacific Rim cuisine. Award-winning celebrated chef Peter Merriman, part owner of Hula Grill, one of the top grossing restaurants on Maui, is considered a culinary pioneer.

Once called "the pied piper of Hawaii regional cuisine" by the Los Angles Times, Merriman teamed up with restaurant entrepreneur Rob Thibaut in 1984 to open the enormously successful Hula Grill, the Hawaii-themed restaurant just steps from Ka'anapali Beach.

The grill replaced the old El Crab Catcher restaurant, still fondly recalled because tables were grouped around a decent-sized swimming pool. Our young kids splashed there as we dined.

Thibaut – "a genius and visionary," according to Merriman – provided a '30s Hawaiian-style beach house, including a barefoot bar with palm-thatched tables. Indoors, locals often sit in front of an open kitchen, dining while they watch a flurry of activity in front of them as the well-greased team of chefs cook on gas or wood-fire stoves. Dollops of sauces are artfully dripped on big white plates soon to hold scrumptious creations.

Hula Grill provided an ever-changing array of dishes emphasizing seafood and blending Hawaiian, Japanese and Chinese cooking methods and local products that have come to be known as Hawaii regional cuisine.

Considered the co-founder of the genre, Peter found early success with locally inspired dishes and saw other chefs paying attention and embracing cuisine that the New York

Times has said makes Merriman "a culinary renaissance man." He is, however, concerned about the future of his best suppliers. He feels the survival of farms is threatened by development that could take away acres of green farmland.

"I kinda don't want them to build bigger roads. The threat is we could lose the whole thing (meaning the beauty of Maui) if we are not careful. We have to decide where that limit is. We can't just keep going, going. I might be accused of drawbridge mentality, but so be it," Merriman commented

The entrepreneur is also concerned about the availability of fish. In the old days, "fish were expensive because they were caught by a couple of guys on a boat." Now, even with mass production, fish remain pricey, because Merriman says we are running out.

"We have difficulty getting fish. There is always fish on the market, but a lot of fish is not caught in Hawaii. We are really worried about this," he said.

Growing up in Pittsburgh, Peter acquired his joy of cooking through his mother, a longtime food writer and city editor of the Pittsburgh Press. Starting as an apprentice at 16 and after attending college, Merriman went on to cook in Vermont, Germany and Washington, D.C. before being recruited to the Big Island in the early '80s.

My wife and I met Merriman at a news conference for Maui County Fine and Fresh, a new program of the county Office of Economic Development to encourage people to buy locally produced farm products.

Merriman had a lot to say, indicating he has been an early proponent of working with local farmers, because "when I was young and foolish, I was doing it partly for the environment. Now I know that it is good business." Turning to the lighter side, Merriman was asked about changes in the restaurant business.

"We started out with mostly seafood and steak. We were more Asian when we first opened, and we don't do much stir fry; we now offer more 'land' foods," he said.

Merriman sees changes in patrons, too: "The dining public becomes more sophisticated every year. There are more people who are adventurous and demanding than they used to be."

Also on the lighter side, Peter was asked for suggestions on how to cope with the many tempting food treats at holiday time. He just laughed. "Ask my slim wife.

"If you want to eat, though, try plenty of veggies and salads – but they have to be flavorful. A lot of people send away for mail order beef. It's pretty fat, so you can slice it, eat two ounces and be satisfied. "

When not working, Peter can be found spending time with his three kids, biking in Haiku and cooking. "I love to cook at home and develop recipes and new concepts that the talented chefs in my restaurants can refine, then add to the menus," Merriman remarked.

Today Merriman is a largely silent partner at Hula Grill but alongside the beachfront restaurant he will open in 2017 Monkeypod Kitchen, a companion to Monkeypod Kitchen at the Wailea resort. The good news for visitors will be that it will offer another choice for the crowds to flock to along Ka'anapali Beach.

OLD TIMER
Sammy Kadotani
OK, OK, the Man Who Can't Say No

IF YOU LIKE THE WORD "OK," you would have loved the late Sammy Kadotano. The 91-year-old community treasure who was described years ago as a "perpetual motion machine" was persistent in using the word "OK" all the time. As a matter of fact, he is persistent in everything, whether it was buying a house or asking for a contribution for his latest cause.

In his distinctive talk story way, Sammy described his first adventure with home ownership.

SAMMY: "There was this house they were building. It was a sample home. I said, 'What the hell, I have to start looking for a home.' I fell in love with that. It was right on Wainee Street further down from the Catholic church.

    "Finally, I came home and said, 'OK, I made up my mind; we are going to buy that house.' It was a three-bedroom. The wife asked, 'Where are we going get the money??' I was working at the Pioneer Mill office for $250 a month. That is OK. I will try to go to the bank. The banker was Jack Vockrodt."

The conversation, according to Sammy, went like this:

BANKER: "OK, Sammy, come on it. You want to buy a house? How much does it cost?"

SAMMY: "$9,600."

BANKER: "OK, come back tomorrow."

SAMMY: "So I went back, and I sat down."

BANKER: "I want all your expenses. Do you drink?" "Yeah. I drink." "How are you going to pay me? You do not have enough."

SAMMY: "I will never forget this: fifty-seven dollars and 72 cents a month (would be the payment)."

BANKER: "OK, you come back tomorrow."

SAMMY: "I must have gone back to see him about 15 times. And he never gave me that answer... finally, the contractor said, 'Sammy, are you going to buy the house? I have to paint the house.' "

SAMMY: "So I said, 'OK. I will try one more time.' So I went down to the bank."

BANKER: "You tell him wait to paint. You come back tomorrow."

Disgusted, Sammy told the banker he would take his business elsewhere.

BANKER: "OK, OK. I will approve that."

SAMMY: "And then I had to borrow $2,000 from my mother. I paid her off slowly, and it took 15 years. When Raymond, my son, finished Lahainaluna, the loan was paid off."

In the early days, Sammy had a chance to take over his father's fish store on Front Street. He wanted no part of it, since as a kid, he could be found usually chopping fish rather than playing baseball. Instead, he became a timekeeper for the mill, showing a talent for management. One if his six bosses once suggested he take a job running the Hotel Hana, but he declined.

His next assignment was to manage Pioneer Hospital, run by the mill. When the hospital closed, doctors formed the Maui Medical Group. Sammy came along to run that. And when Kaiser Permanente came in to build a clinic, Sammy moved over there to run that for 13 years, too.

Sammy's other talent was raising money for every conceivable cause. His mind for dates may not be what it once was, but he remembeed every project and every idea he put into action.

He pushed to get Lahaina a community swimming pool, raised money for a $15,000 electronic scoreboard for Lahainaluna High School, and in 1987, he ran a Lahaina community reunion that attracted 3,000 people.

In 1994, he formed the PGA (Proud Grandparents Association) to raise funds for King Kamehameha III grammar school. He decided that it should have a statue of the great king to commemorate the school's 100th birthday. He signed on a sculptor and raised $5,000 to help pay for it.

Lahaina Restoration Foundation needed to sell bricks to finance the restoration of the Pioneer Mill Co. Smokestack. With Sammy in charge, LRF sold more than 1,000.

An avid golfer, Sammy played at Ka'anapali in the 1960s for $12 a round. He quit golf because it became too expensive, but not before playing in "Swinging with Sammy," a golf tournament for locals he organized that continued for 20 years.

No profile of Sammy is complete without mentioning boats. With friends, he used to remove the metal from old plantation house roofs to make tin boats to ride out to the waves. The kids used washboards as surfboards.

His front yard features a canoe once used in the Spencer Tracy film "The Devil at Four O'clock," which was filmed in Lahaina. Painted on the side is *"E komo mai"* (welcome).

Among Sammy's proudest achievements and highlights of a long life was his first trip to the Mainland, bringing along 21 Boy Scouts to a national Jamboree in Colorado and traveling for six weeks by plane, train, automobile and bus.

Pride in his sons and grandsons was also a highlight. The Kadotani's put two sons through college. Raymond runs Take Home Maui, the "pineapple store" on Dickenson Street, and Owen worked for years as a chef at Ka'anapali resorts before opening a business.

A grandson graduated from law school, and a granddaughter works in human relations for Hula Grill.

Sammy's favorite relaxation would be watching the San Francisco 49ers. A fanatic, he taped all the games and watched them again and again. He still couldn't get over a Super Bowl loss and "the terrible call by a referee.

"I've watched it three times. And they lose every time!"

Over the years, his wife, Hatsumi, has tried to get him to go to the beach more. "But he just can't stop," Sammy said.

He summed up his own life best: "I like to help. People say, 'Hey Sammy.' I can't tell them no. When do you want me?"

REALTOR
Bob Cartwright
Learning the Value of Aloha

OVER THE YEARS, it could be argued, a Chart House cook transferred from California to Maui, who later became a waiter, has become the most influential and successful real estate broker on Maui. He's affable, astute Bob Cartwright, co-owner with wife Tess of Whalers Realty Inc., the largest independent real estate firm on the West Side.

In the business of helping people enjoy the benefits of Maui, as he puts it, the hardworking Cartwright has been watching and participating in the mostly ups — and sometimes downs — of West Side real estate over three decades.

Transitioning into real estate from the restaurant business, Cartwright secured a real estate license when a partner at Whalers Realty recognized his potential and offered to bankroll a real estate licensing course for him.

Cartwright joined the company he and his wife Tess would one day acquire in 1983. His start with Whalers began in the office of Jack Kelley, one of Whalers Realty's four partners. A short but sweet hiring interview went this way, Bob reported:

KELLEY: "I hear you want to work for us, and I like the fact that you have a track record representing developers on new projects. I hear you are pretty good. I think you could make a contribution. But let me tell you how it works around here. If you ever come into my office and ask me a question, you are fired."

CARTWRIGHT:
   "I'm a big boy. I think I can handle that."

KELLEY: "Well, get the hell out of here. You're hired."

In 1981, Bob had met Tess Hallmark, an artist, on a cruise ship off Hawaii Island. He was there on business, and she was drawing caricatures, dabbling in real estate and looking for someone to dance with.

The two joined Whalers Realty together and began running ads using the phrase, "Ask for the Best," patterned after the biblical phrase "ask and thou shalt receive" to distinguish themselves from other agents.

Kelley, in ill health, later sold them the firm in 1993. Soon, "Ask for the Best" became the slogan of the entire company and applied to all of its agents, who now gather to shout it out in TV commercials.

Fast growth brought Whalers Realty from six agents in the early 1980's to 35 at the peak under the Cartwrights' ownership and sales of at least $100 million a year. Agents during this tougher market now number 24.

For one of his clients, Cartwright has bought and sold a whopping 25 purchases — some transitional, some for investment.

The most pleasurable achievement for Maui brokers, he said, is helping people realize the benefits of living on Maui.

Mellowing after years in the business, riding the peaks and valleys as real estate soared or collapsed, Cartwright's philosophy is that what Realtors do is not so much sell real estate but helping people with transitions in their lives.

It starts with what the broker calls "the thrill of helping the first-time buyer." It then moves on to helping find a larger home when a new baby arrives and finally putting a retired couple into a retirement dream home. Or, in a less pleasant instances in between, helping a relocated divorcee.

"I've watched people's health improve when they move here," he said. Cartwright's top five benefits: better health, learning aloha, enjoying natural beauty, pursuing of the intellectual and spiritual, and the happiness of owning a home in paradise.

"Research has shown that due to our weather and lifestyle, people live longer and happier lives on Maui than anywhere else. "Learning the meaning and then living in the spirit of ALOHA by honoring the noblest attributes of our host Hawaiian culture is one of our greatest benefits," he said.

"There is also the ability every day to appreciate and enjoy nature, and the ability to grow and mature through a plethora of opportunities available through community groups and organizations.

"And finally the happiness that springs from the security of owning a home in this beautiful and special place," he added.

Blackie Gadarian, a machinist by trade, crafted ironwork for the Hyatt, the hotel built along the beach, and later opened a famous bar .

SIX
REMARKABLE PEOPLE HERE and ABOUT

Aloha is a two-way street. If you are nice, we are nice.

—Octogenarian Blackie Gadarian

GADFLY
Blackie Gadarian
A Boatyard and a Bar

THE BEST WORD TO DESCRIBE ORANGE-SHIRT-ED Blackie Gadarian—90-year-old machinist, former bar owner, jazz buff, and irascible writer of pithy letters to local publications—is colorful.

Growing up in New York City, Arsene Gadarian won the moniker "Blackie" because of his thick black hair (now entirely gone).

After World War II, Blackie started Blackie's Boatyard in Newport Beach, California, later opening a second one on Maui in 1979. To paint his new boat-maintenance buildings in California, struggling Blackie got some strange, lead-based red paint for free. A year later it turned an ugly color, and Blackie was told the only new color he could paint over it was orange.

The orange buildings became a trademark and orange shirts followed, worn the last 29 years on Maui. (His closet now has 40 of them, and none of another color.) Wife Sara drives him around in an orange golf cart and truck with an orange stripe and logo. Sara usually wears light-blue shirts.

Blackie is most famous around these parts for Blackie's Bar, an infamous hangout on land that once stood in the middle of his boatyard near the current Shell station across from Lahaina Cannery Mall.

To build his bar, the innovative Blackie bought the top of Windsock Lounge, well known as the place to go have a drink before boarding a plane at the old West Maui Airport at Airport Beach in Ka'anapali.

Blackie wanted the bar, which he put on a truck and hauled to Lahaina, because it was the stomping ground of renowned bartender "High School Harry" Given, revered for his powerful Bloody Mary's. Blackie's Bar kept the Bloody Mary's and also added Sara's famous, home-cooked meat-loaf sandwich ($5.50).

The colorful Blackie sprang from colorful parents—two Armenian guerilla fighters who had to fight their way out of Turkey to come to New York. Born in 1921, Blackie grew up at 23rd Street and Third Avenue in Manhattan, as well as on the edge of Harlem.

During the height of the Depression, he took five-cent subway rides to a trade school, where he learned to be a machinist. After a first job in which he said he earned 11 cents an hour, he joined the US Navy at the start of World War II. As an airplane mechanic, he served on carrier flight decks in the Pacific and also spent time in Hawaii.

Blackie apparently was somewhat of a hellion. When he tried to reenlist after the war, the US Navy said it was willing to take him back only if he would accept a demotion. Blackie said no. For the next 20 years, the talented machinist worked on aircraft maintenance for Western Airlines in Los Angeles and a company serving private airplanes. Next came the boatyards in Newport and Maui.

Blackie's Boatyard, highly visible along Honoapi'ilani Highway, was on a landlocked industrial lot far from the water. While the yard never did well, the adjoining machine shop prospered thanks to a hotel construction boom. A good customer was the new Hyatt Regency Maui, with West Maui's only machinist supplying brass railings, parrot cages, and other ornamentals.

Then in 1981 came the bar, started for fun. Blackie's love of jazz—acquired in the days when he hung out at Harlem's famous Apollo Theater—encouraged him to turn the bar into a popular music venue. Jazz music buffs began flocking to the bar four nights a week to hear top artists, including the likes of George Benson and others who would sit in with local groups.

Blackie's was a no-nonsense bar. You couldn't stop with just a drink and a meal. If you wanted to stay, you had to buy another drink and another. Blackie said so, claiming he did not want tourists lingering at tables. Fail to comply, and you would be escorted out.

"Many people today claim they were thrown out of my bar. I actually only threw out six," Blackie said. (One was his brother.) Blackie's Bar closed more than 20 years ago. But Maui had not heard the last of Blackie.

GADARIAN REVISITED
Blackie Gadarian
It's Blackie Against the World

SOFT-SPOKEN SARA RICHARDSON GADARIAN has been married to "lovable, humble Blackie" for 48 years.

When they met, she said, "I saw a feisty man—tall, dark, and handsome. He had a wonderful sense of humor. He made me laugh, and he loved music and the beach. And he was a wonderful dancer who could do the Lindy Hop."

The marriage has survived, in part, because Sara—owner of an infectious laugh—has a sense of humor, too.

Behind the rough, gruff, facade of the former Lahaina bar owner Arsene "Blackie" Gadarian is "a man who is extremely gentle with the people he loves," Sara said. "But usually it is Blackie against the world."

Many KPOA listeners were introduced to humble Blackie by radio commercials featuring the iconoclast himself. "Blackie's Bar is for grownups. Leave your kids and dogs at the hotel. This is your wonderful, lovable, humble Blackie," he would say.

Visitors to the beer, burger, and jazz joint just north of town were first accosted by a special sign.

Blackie explained, "Most tourists used to be told that the streets of Lahaina were lined with free coupons. And everything was aloha. We had a sign that said, 'Aloha is a two-way street.' If you come here and are nice, we are nice. If you come here and are (unprintable), we will be (unprintable)." Above a long stairway lined with photos of old shipwrecks, there were more signs and more rules:

PROMOTE SAFE BOATING.
STAY ASHORE AND DRINK AT BLACKIE'S BAR!
*

NO PIPE OR CIGAR SMOKING PERMITTED.
*

KEEP YOUR FEET AND LEGS OFF THE CHAIRS.
*

IF YOU ARE NOT DRINKING, YOU ARE LOITERING!

Blackie's own drinking was supposed to be legendary, but he had a trick up his orange sleeve. Customers would buy him drinks, and he would pour the contents down a convenient drain when they weren't looking. He claims his other secret was that having more than two drinks actually made him sick.

On jazz nights, Blackie would open the show with a monologue. Now, with the bar closed since 1991, he's taken to baiting tourists—he does not call them "visitors"—many evenings at Leilani's on the Beach at Whalers Village Shopping Center.

Blackie, with a cane, and Sara stroll in. Bar patrons scatter, and the two get stools. "What else am I going to do? I am not going to sit home and throw bread to the birds," said Blackie.

Outrageous things come out of Blackie's mouth all the time—best left unchallenged. Yet, for anyone who loves to debate issues, the cantankerous Blackie is a joy. Once he has accepted you, he's fun to talk to, because he is well informed and a self-described "news junkie."

Obama? "If he can't stop smoking, how is he going to stop the war?" Development? "We have people who gripe about too much development. 'It is too crowded.' When I was born, there were 120 million people in the country. Now there are 300 million—what are we going to do?"

Blackie Gadarian in his early nineties spent his time writing of pithy, short letters to the editor in local newspapers and visiting his favorite bar which seemed to change every other month.

When and if he reaches the pearly gates, he must consider one thing: "No loitering." Blackie got the chance to see whether than applied. He passing away in 2013.

PASTOR
Laki Pomaikai
From green fields to saving souls

NINE-YEAR-OLD LAKI POMAIKAI already looked like a loser. Today, he may be the most flamboyant, colorful preacher in all of Maui.

His father drank, and his family was impoverished. "I watched my father steal a can of Spam. My father literally tied ropes around our house to keep it from collapsing. I was an alcoholic at age nine," he told his flock of visitors and locals at Sunday services.

The example of his father signaled to Laki that stealing was OK. The future man of God became what he calls "an accomplished thief" in a pamphlet titled From Green Fields of Marijuana to Prison Greens.

The boy who drank and grew up near St. Theresa Church in Kihei would go on to serve in the jungles of Vietnam after high school. Returning home, he was arrested in the eighties for growing 800 marijuana plants. He got five years in prison.

Paroled, he later got caught selling cocaine. A judge at the time threw the book at him—a 50-year sentence, minimum of 10 years.

And then, a kind of miracle happened. Laki found religion. Behind closed walls 23 out of 24 hours, he had plenty of time to read the Bible, which he now quotes liberally and knowledgeably. His conversion came from within, he said.

Demonstrating his sincerity, he was let go after just 22 months and immediately began religious training at the Cleveland, Tennessee, headquarters of a Pentecostal Christian denomination, the Church of God. (The church has seven million members in 170 countries and one million followers in the United States.)

The Pomakai family had fallen a long way. Laki claims he is the great great grandson of Queen Kaʻahumanu, favorite wife of King Kamehameha the Great. He even adopted a new name: Laki Pomakai Kaʻahumanu. However, the queen never had any children, at least that we know of.

Pillars of the community say this heritage is true. Following religious training, the Vietnam veteran has not looked back.

In fact, one of his many missions is slipping From Green Fields under jail-cell doors at the county prison in Wailuku on regular visits. He shows inmates, through his own life, that they can change. Laki numbers many converts.

Another place he can be found is near the beaches of Ka'anapali and Kapalua. Visitors and locals learn that they can tie the knot and be married overlooking the beach or anywhere.

The pastor performs numerous ceremonies a year. Purists may question the ceremony's authenticity, but Laki said it meets the needs of people who do not want to be married in a church.

A conch shell is blown, a chant given, rings and *lei* are exchanged, and a blessing bestowed.

With Maili, his wife of 29 years, Pastor Laki has sponsored 21 hanai (adopted) children over a period of decades, taking them in from broken homes, nurturing them, and sending them on their way. Many have risen up from nothing, like him.

As pastor of Harvest Chapel on Prison Street and a church in Lana'i City, Pastor Laki also provided refuge and shelter to battered women, homeless women with children, and the underprivileged and disadvantaged.

Over the last decade, he also spent two years in Las Vegas ministering there.

Today, he preaches at his Church on the Go, holding chapel services each Sunday at 8:00 a.m. at the Kaanapali Beach Hotel. There, he asks visitors to say where they are from and why they are thankful to God. He plays a religious song on ukulele and offers stories filled with biblical references.

The reaction to his flamboyant style is positive. Two visitors who heard about him at a luau the night before said, "The luau was wonderful, but this was the best part of our trip."

Chris Pietzsch, a neighbor of Laki's from Kula, allowed that "he speaks from the heart. I have never seen anyone like him. He's genuine."

Joe Pluta, a close friend, calls Laki a "Mighty Man of God, whose number-one priority is to serve God! He has accomplished many miracles in his life and is a living inspiration."

At one service, Laki talks about hell, writes the word on a piece of paper, and tears it into pieces after dropping it to the ground. Someone nearby picks it up to take home.

After the service, Laki gathers in a circle around a cancer patient and her family. Comfort is provided, tears are shed, and hugs exchanged.

"My job is to edify you—build you up," he tells visitors. And then he ends with an interpretation of aloha: A (always), L (love), O (over), H (hate), A (always).

To that, we can say only Amen.

HULA DANCER
Kalea Jaramillo
Marring a Man on the Way to Jail

WHEN THE FUTURE Mrs. Kalei Jaramillo attended court to see her longtime boyfriend sentenced to seven years in prison for dealing drugs, no one expected he would be taken immediately to jail. And so he cried out to the judge, "Marry us."

The judge asked if anyone objected. No one did. And so Kalele became Mrs. Kalei Jaramillo. The considerate judge asked if anyone had a camera to photograph the newlywed couple. Someone did and snapped pictures. Kalele kissed him good-bye and then he was taken away.

The couple embarked on years of suffering, he in jail on Maui and then in Arizona where the state houses some its prisoners, and she in Lahaina, carrying out ordinary, productive days all the while suffering from her husband's absence.

The couple is still waiting for a honeymoon and to consummate their marriage since no conjugal visits are allowed in Arizona, where Jaramillo has spent four of the last seven jailed years.

Every Sunday the lovely Kalele, a kumu hula dances at Pastor Laki's Church on the Go in Ka'anapali. And there is always a hug and a kiss for the columnist who has been thinking about writing about the couple for a long time in part because an injustice is being done.

Kalele noted that she is not very comfortable talking about herself. Both she and her husband have been through many traumas they now seem to have overcome them. She prefers that the traumas remain unnamed.

Kalele shares a birthday card that she keeps in her purse from her husband, a talented artist. He drew a beautiful rose on the sheet. Clearly, his message to her and what she says about the boy she has known since childhood who's now a man clearly show they are very much in love. "He has a good heart," she volunteers. "He believes in God."

Kalele grew up on Maui, graduating from Kamehameha III Elementary and Lahainaluna High School where she was a cheerleader. More years ago than she can remember she learned hula from the legendary Emma Sharpe, joining dozens of others who still dance in the Auntie Emma style at resorts and even political rallies to this day.

She danced as a child at both the Sheraton Maui and the Kapa Room at the old Maui Surf (now the Westin). She remembers being taken out for ice cream afterwards at Ed and Dons. And she has danced in Japan and Korea where there are lot of people who love hula.

She is also fond of dancing Polynesian and Samoan style and even took up belly dancing the first time she saw it, taught by a new friend. And if not enough, she has a license and sometimes marries people. She can also dance with fire! Kalele dances twice a week at Hula Grill, teaches hula at the Napili Kai Resort, and often dances at the airport for arriving visitors on Fridays. "I like to bring happiness to people," she explains.

When not working, she pretty much stays home, sometimes enjoying video visits with her husband between trips to Arizona where she can hold hands with him for as long as eight hours a day during a visit.

What has brought both through these last years has been their faith. "I am a spiritual person," Kalele says. "Every day when I wake up, I think today is the day my husband is going to be released. You do what you have to do. She know how long he has been away in years, months and days at any given time.

The injustice has been handed out by the parole board. Although sentenced to seven years by a Maui judge who heard all the evidence, the parole board extended his sentence to 15 years.

One wonders what they could possibly be thinking especially because he has become more deeply religious, hoping to return to Maui one day to make amends by voluntarily doing community service and helping young people. Meanwhile, the State of Hawaii continues to pay Arizona to keep him in prison.

Kalele makes a living through dancing and gives private hula lessons for pay. She sometimes teaches brides how to hula so they can surprise their new husbands on their wedding night.

A friend who has known her for many years noted Kalele is a wonderful person. Clearly this couple when united deserves better.

MODERN-DAY WHALERS
Flip Nicklin, Ed Lyman
Whale Soup

"IT IS WHALE SOUP OUT HERE," beamed Captain Jung of the Hawaii Ocean Project. The captain led a recent whale watch for Whale Trust Maui, the pioneering group whose members have taught us more about whale behavior in the past 20 years than what was learned in the last 200.

Some 175 years ago, the cry "thar she blows" could be heard across the Pacific as whalers from New England harpooned and killed thousands of sperm whales for the oil for lamps that would light thousands of homes before power from electricity.

Lahaina was one of the whaling capitals of the world, provisioning ships that roamed the Pacific and providing diversion for whaling crews away for months. Some 500 whaling ships a year visited these shores.

Today, Lahaina is another whaling capital: the capital of worldwide research on these majestic creatures now protected who visit us each year in numbers approaching 10,000.

The whales cavort and have babies, and whale researchers return each year to tell us what they have learned in a two-day forum.

Researchers like Meagan Jones-Gray who has the look of a movie star and the pioneering Jim Darling who has been studying whales here for 30 years are joined by two special people who have different missions.

For Charles "Flip" Nicklin—today widely regarded as the premier whale photographer in the world according to National Geographic—the connection with these massive giants of the sea goes way back.

Ed Lyman never met an entangled humpback whale, loaded down with fishing gear or marine debris, he didn't want to rescue, free, and help to swim loose.

When Flip (nicknamed after a character in the 1940s comic strip "Terry and the Pirates") left his father's dive shop in San Diego for Maui decades back, he sought adventure and a way to make a living.

Flip's great-great-grandfather arrived on the West Coast on a whaling ship. His father, who he has always called "Chuck" was not only a dive-shop owner but a world-class cinematographer who came to Maui 1n 1976 for a shoot."

Flip as a young man tagged along as a deckhand on a whale research ship and was mentored by National Geographic ace underwater photographers Bates Littlehales and Jonathan Blair, who taught him about lenses and light.

Flip took photos alongside them and, as a beginning photographer, got three of his photos published in the magazine. This was a follow-up to the $10 he received from a kids' magazine for his first published photo.

Flip may flip over when he is on one of his 60-second dives, but he has never flipped careers. He has been photographing whales and dolphins since 1976 for fun and pay.

In free dives as deep as 100 feet, Flip takes several deep breaths and has just 60 seconds under water to click off his photos. One of 500 shots is a keeper, he told some 200 people at a recent Whale Trust Maui talk story session.

By free diving with only a small air tank for emergencies, the free-diving photographer generates no bubbles "that would change the whole human to whale dynamic," he wrote in the handsomely illustrated book "Among Giants: A Life with Whales."

Flip often partners with research pioneer Jim Darling in a three-boat armada of sorts. Darling has "the singing boat," because he researches whale songs. Meagan Jones-Gray, one of the Whale Trust Maui founders with Nicklin, operates out of the "female boat" for research on the behavior of female whales. Flip and videographers work out of "the video boat."

The whale's journey to the Lahaina Channel from Alaska begins in late fall. Not far behind is Nicklin who perhaps appropriately makes his home in Alaska as well.

Another "modern whaler" is Ed Lyman, untangler of whales.

The history of entangling whales dates to the seventies. Lyman has rescued some 70 whales up in their Alaskan home.

In the early rescue days, control lines were first affixed that led to the famous Nantucket sleigh ride—a whale pulling a boat at rapid speeds when harpooned.

It turns out that whales regard Lahaina as their own paradise, but entangled whales can be found in places from Newfoundland to Tonga, Alaska to Australia. Some 80 entangled whales have been rescued in Newfoundland alone.

When Lyman and others expanded their mission from Alaska in summer to Hawaii in winter, they found what Lyman calls "a magical environment." Assisting him, he said, were people with the spirit of aloha. He indicated he has never been anywhere where the cooperation of seamen has been so great.

Techniques have changed. Now the rescue teams use a "flying knife" of hardened steel to cut entangling lines. The poles and their control lines can be as long as 35 feet and are sometimes made from ship's masts. The latest innovation is cameras, two to provide a three-dimensional look placed near the cutting point to make possible easy vision and a clean cut.

Sometimes, said Lyman, as he scanned the sea on a Whale Trust whale watch, "you have to make sure you do not slip off the boat."

When freed, some whales zoom away at breakneck speed. Others dally, perhaps not knowing they are free.

As to man's experience with whales, there has been a sea change. In Tonga, inhabitants once hunted whales. Now they work to save the entangled creatures.

Today, the great thing is that humpbacks and other whales do not have to contend with tough characters like the fictional Captain Ahab. And no longer do they have to fear the cry made famous by Herman Melville: "Thar she blows!"

STORYTELLER
Kekoa Mowat
Tale of Kaʻanapali

FIVE HUNDRED YEARS AGO, Kekaʻa village, with 10,000 souls, stretched from today's North Beach beyond the old Airport Beach, all the way to Canoe Beach below the Hyatt Regency Maui Resort and Spa.

There was no beach named Kaʻanapali. One of the world's greatest, most famous beaches was known to Hawaiians as Kekaʻa, a name that survives only on the curving road down the hill from Honoapiʻilani Highway to Kaʻanapali.

The real Kaʻanapali was farther north, but resort developers liked the romantic name so much they renamed Kekaʻa as Kaʻanapali, according to Kekoa Mowat and Krislyn Lavey, tour guides extraordinaire. This little secret is just one of the tales told as part of the two-year-old Kaʻanapali Historical

Trail and Legends Guided Tour for locals and visitors sponsored by the Kaʻanapali Beach Resort Association.

Boarding the Kaʻanapali trolley, wearing walking shoes for strolls where sugarcane-plantation camps once filled the landscape, locals and visitors alike joined guide Kekoa and his partner in a two-hour journey into history. Legends came to life as the rich history of those who walked these sands before us was explained with verve and enthusiasm.

Listen as tour guide Kekoa explains, "The pie-shaped village of Kekaʻa from the outer reefs through fertile lands extended all the way to the mountains. *Hoʻokipa,* the constant generous sharing of food and resources was the way of life." Fish brought from the sea were shared with people above who had bananas, sweet potatoes or other fruits of the land.

Medicinal plants or wood for canoes or spears harvested from higher elevations were constantly exchanged for *limu* (seaweed) or shellfish gathered on shorelines where newcomers now stroll.

Thatched huts where kupuna watched children while their fathers and mothers worked stretched to the horizon in a self-contained district where a proud and industrious people shared freely of what they had.

Children were often the product of temporary unions, with the motive of bringing forth children who would be of a higher class. "Kind of like the sixties," Kekoa noted.

Overlooking the Royal Kaʻanapali Golf Course, Kekoa and Krislyn acted out the legend of Moe Moe. Responding to requests by his mother, whose tapa for cloth making was not curing fast enough, the demigod Maui journeys to the peak of Haleakala to snare the sun and bring it across island to dry the tapa. Maui asks his human friend, Moe Moe, for help, but Moe Moe prefers sleep. Maui turns him into a large flat, now sacred stone.

The huge stone sat in peace for centuries, if not eons, until the building of Ka'anapali Resort. The heavy, sacred rock is pulled by machine from a hole for a swimming pool. The next morning, it mysteriously is back in the hole. Two more times it is removed.

After each night, it turns up back in the hole. Modern man gets the message. The stone is carefully placed in a new location with a clear view of the sea and a special blessing ceremony held. More than 30 years later, the stone of Moe Moe sits in the same place, back to sleep.

According to Hawaiian values, it is important for people to have a sense of place, explained Moloka'i-born Kekoa, through the telling of legends and exploration of history. "We were never taught about our culture or the history of Lahaina in school. We're doing this now so students and locals can get more knowledge about places we pass by every day," he explained.

After growing up on the beach in Moloka'i, boarding at Lahainaluna High School, and playing football—"We lost the championship game even though we were up 14–0 with a few minutes to play"—Kekoa graduated in 1988 and then stayed after marrying his Maui-born high-school sweetheart.

He joined the Hyatt, moving up to the post of director of security and safety and having his boss volunteer him for the guide program. To prepare for this story telling Kekoa took 40 hours of classes in Hawaiian culture from the community college and even got drama lessons to help him act out the legends. The preparation served his audience well.

AUTHOR
Norm Bezane
A Nostalgic Look Back at 27 Years as a Visitor

MAINLANDERS often fondly remember summers at the lake. Our family from Chicago waxes nostalgic about decades of vacationing on Maui before we, as parents, became permanent residents in 2001.

This reminiscence, taking a look back at the ever-changing Maui scene as experienced from a visitor's perspective, offers a glimpse of how Maui has changed, and how, in some respects, it remains the same.

Forty years ago, when the world-famous Ka'anapali Beach Resort was a onetime dream destination for legions of bubbly honeymooners and visitors on seven-day package tours, those with that first-time-in-paradise glow didn't think about returning.

Our kids were an exception, returning on vacation with us nearly 27 years in the seventies, eighties, and nineties and as grownups in the new millennium.

They stepped foot on Maui for the first the time from Hawaiian Airlines planes that then debarked people right on the tarmac before there were jet ways. Over the years they rode in "umbrella" strollers, toddled across rope bridges, sailed on catamarans, and floated over Ka'anapali on a parasail. As they grew older, they returned as adults.

These days, visitors arrive at the fairly cosmopolitan Kahului airport. In those early years, you hopped on Hawaiian Air on Oahu after a trip from the mainland and deplaned to walk to a sleepy baggage-claim area, picking up your bags.

Today, from our bulging photo album, spring forth not only photos of our "Ka'anapali Kids" but the remarkable evolution of one of the world's best-planned and workable resorts—a resort that no longer is the exclusive paradise for just newlyweds and first-time tourists.

Now, as the ads say, "the world comes to play," and Ka'anapali Kids once so rare can now can be found on every beach and around every corner, many on return trips.

Paging through the family album not only brings back memories of the decades on Ka'anapali, it brings the realization that we have more photos of our kids' two-week sojourns to Ka'anapali (often each Easter) than from the 50 weeks we spent annually at home in Chicago.

And there are even some from Honolulu, including one memorable frame taken when an entertainer we remember as "Sonia" picked our baby up and sang to her at the old Garden Bar at the Hilton Hawaiian Village.

The first night our six-month-old daughter stayed away from home was spent at the Kahana Sunset even before there was a Kapalua just up the road. Evenings were enjoyed in Ka'anapali or Lahaina, with our daughter frequently tucked in a stroller sleeping under a restaurant table somewhere while we dined on ahi.

Given our daughter's continuing ability to fall asleep easily anywhere, we used to say that our young traveler had slept at all the best restaurants in Lahaina, including Kimo's and even outside the fancier Longhi's Restaurant, parked on the sidewalk below a big open window. We dined just inside to the amusement—in those days—of not-so-frequent passersby.

Though we are still lean people, a lot of the photos and memories revolve around eating. At our usual 5:00 a.m. jet-lagged awakening on a first day in Maui, we evolved a tradition of driving to the Hyatt (then called a hotel and not a resort) for an early walk through the Japanese garden. The garden has not changed in all these years.

This would be followed by pineapple pancakes in Lahaina Town at historic Pioneer Inn overlooking the harbor. Once or twice a trip we would return, broiling our own cook-yourself dinners in the interior courtyard (mahi, seven minutes).

The cook-your-own barbecue pit is no more, as are most of the hundreds of whaling artifacts on the wall of the bar within view of a fleet of fishing boats. Now only a few remain.

The broil-your-own concept was also a staple at the Old Rusty Harpoon, now gone after a move to a new location that led to its demise.

We'd grill our own burgers—some of the best we've ever tasted—against a backdrop of fresh sea air and Moloka'i in the distance. Another favorite spot was the old Crab Catcher restaurant, predecessor to today's popular Hula Grill at Whalers Village Shopping Center, centerpiece of the resort area right on the ocean.

Besides scrumptious nachos unlike any to be found today—so it seems—the Crab Catcher featured a small swimming pool where our kids could wade or swim while we ate hamburgers (we both still ate meat and had better teeth in those days).

Also remembered fondly was the nearby Chico's, the place for tacos before anyone had ever heard of Maui Tacos.

It was at Whalers Village that I once left our newborn son in a stroller in the aisle of the old bookstore next to the Rusty Harpoon, only to leave and then remember that we had had a second child and he had been left behind. (He was still there, fast asleep alongside the Hawaiiana book section.)

And then there were daily visits to Yami Yogurt for a product so good we wished we could get it in Chicago and nearby Ricco's, the cozy open-air pizza place where a "new" air-conditioned fast-food court now stands. Both have been casualties of progress.

Our Ka'anapali Kids did more than eat and stay on the beach. We'd go to the community Easter-egg hunt under the Banyan Tree in town each year, with our son one time finding the golden egg entitling him to a special prize, a canister of Play-Doh. And of course there was Easter-egg coloring at three different resorts and the Makawao Rodeo on the Fourth of July.

There were family milestones too. One life-changing event oc-curred on the curving golf course lined pathway along Ka'anapali Parkway one evening in 1981. My wife, Sara, and I made a life-changing decision that one of us would quit work.

In the days when it was rare for husband and wife to both have demanding careers with two kids, it was along Ka'anapali Parkway that I decided to quit my job as a corporate publications manager and stay home as one of the earliest househusbands.

Today, passing by now almost daily, I remember the walkway fondly since the decision there, it turned out, was one of the most rewarding ones I have ever made.

One blustery day on trip number 23, tragedy almost struck. In a first and only use of a video camera, I decided to film an entire day of our favorite family activities, mynas chirping at wakeup, breakfast at Pioneer Inn, a ride on the Ka'anapali Resort trolley, and a day at the beach.

Videotaping away, I was glad to see the enormous and picturesque waves that my wife and kids plunged into for "the ocean shot." Problem was my wife got in trouble, saved only by the fact that our daughter had become a good swimmer. Our 39-year-old refuses to look at the video to this day.

Our Ka'anapali Kids are no longer kids now but

they still keep coming back from Chicago and New York to what we sometimes called "Conorpali Beach." We used to say to our young son Conor that one day he would own one of the houses behind the colorful rows of azaleas facing Honoapiʻilani Highway in front of Kaʻanapali Beach Resort.

He doesn't own one yet but you never know. But his Kaʻanapali parents now own a permanent residence close by up the hill from Kaʻanapali not far away. Since 2001, we've learned that living on Maui is far different than visiting.

We came from a big city, and this is a small town. One of us—not me—thought we'd get "island fever," a fear that a small island would not be enough to keep us happy and busy.

Visitors often ask if we came to get away from cold weather. Not really. We came for the deep-blue skies with white billowing clouds, the warm ocean, the lush forests, plumeria, the aloha, and, we have come to realize, the remarkable people

Alas, we have found that music is everywhere, almost every weekend brings a festival and the days are so packed with work or community-related activities that visits to the beach become rarer and rarer.

And we have the Maui Arts & Cultural Center, one of several venues around the world where voters see Academy-Award-nominated movies in December and concerts by the Beach Boys, Fleetwood Mac, and others.

In recent years, as volunteers, we have learned what a wonderful community Lahaina is. In 2011, Sara, my wife, spearheaded modernization of the Lahaina Public Library without public expense. Some 21 contractors and service providers donated $150,000 worth of free work.

Some 80 residents and visitors packed up 35,000 books and emptied the library to prepare for the revitalization. The spirit of volunteerism was infectious.

Meanwhile we have seen a revolution in technology that makes it possible for many professionals to live here and do their work through the Internet. Our digital-photo file has grown to 27,000 images, and this does not count the hundreds and hundreds made with a film camera in the last century.

Visitors we meet often frequently ask if we are retired. The answer is, "not really. "The public relations business we started has wound down, but we are having the time of lives writing, and producing a photo blog called "Joys of Ka'anapali."

Before serving as the president of a condominium association, Sara had started a community project to landscape the front lawn of the library with Native Hawaiian plants that better showcase the history of the monarchs when this was the capital of the Hawaiian Islands.

Years ago, in the Midwest, family memories of many people used to revolve around summers at the lake. Ours are filled with fond memories of Ka'anapali Beach and Lahaina, as they will in the years ahead for increasing numbers of Ka'anapali Kids building new traditions on the greatest place on earth. Maybe someday they will even end up living here, becoming voices of aloha too.

LOYAL FRIEND
Kea Aloha
Day in Life of Kea Aloha

AS THE ONLY NATIVE HAWAIIAN in our family, born in Hilo, Hawaii, weaned in Honolulu on Sand Island, arriving on Maui via Hawaiian Air just three months after birth, Kea Aloha loves living in the greatest place on earth.

The white fluffy guy is very frequently petted by visitors who miss their animals and love this dog.

The vet has said he has a very strong heart. That's because his masters walk him down and then up Keka'a Drive hill every morning to visit the resorts and sit on a soon-to-be rented beach cabana chair to watch Trilogy snorkel day-trippers depart each morning.

Kea spends more time at the beach than many residents who mostly seem to go to and fro to the store or other places unconnected to the joys of paradise. Kea takes up his story in his own words.

"My first stop in the morning is the KBH valet stand where I say hello to my friends Patti, Bobbie, Clayton, and Ron (who insists I need training). There he is known as 'Mr. White,' for his namesake Mike White, general manager of the hotel.

"To let others dogs know I have been around, I raise my hind leg on my favorite signs, one saying, 'Stop' and another, 'No Parking. Your Car Will Be Towed by Ali'i Towing.' The ocean used to scare me to death, even the sound of it before I could see it. Now it merely frightens me.

"I go to a lot of places, particularly liking the Sunday Drive to Ulupalakua Ranch where I once heard a famous singer appear at the winery. I had to stand outside the white picket fence though. I have even marched in a Whale Day parade.

"My friend Tommy thinks I am a conservative, but as usual 100 percent of the time, he is wrong. I don't like Fox either since I do not like animal channels that put out false 'information.'

"My favorite hangout place is Paia Fish Market where I sit under a picnic table and watch the masters eat ono sandwiches, which they claim are the best on the island. Must they always eat three times a day?

"I have been on vacation to Chicago but the last trip was harrowing. American Airlines was fine without a reservation. But on a second trip on United flying out of Honolulu, a clerk asked for my reservation and I had none. We missed our flight and my owner had to take me in a cab to outside the airport and a freight building, waiting six hours for another flight.

"In the evening, I sometimes go for a run with my friend Parker, a tiny dog who recently broke her leg jumping off a sofa and had to have a metal plate put in. No more incessant ball chasing for her.

"I also sometimes blitz at home around the kitchen counter, the dining table, and sofa when my two-legged friend decides to chase me. I could be a great NFL halfback because of my quick moves since the friend never catches me. A football is too big for me to carry, however.

"I have become famous, though. I am pictured on the Lahaina Library Facelift Timeline blog because I served as a volunteer for the Rotary Club of Lahaina modernization project. And I have been praised in a book for not eating the author's manuscript for breakfast."

Commercial  Advertiser.

Established Oct 2, 1868.

VOL. XXVIII, NO. 4055   HONOLULU, HAWAIIAN ISLANDS, THURSDAY, JULY 14, 1898.   PRICE FIVE CENTS.

ANNEXATION!

CERVERA'S FLEET IS ANNIHILATED

Attempted to Run the Blockade at Santiago.
He Is a Prisoner---Heavy Losses

COMMANDER W. S. SCHLEY.

"HERE TO STAY!"

And the star-spangled banner
In triumph shall wave,
O'er the Isles of Hawaii
And the homes of the brave.

H. M. WHITNEY

FIRST NEWS.

VOTE AT WASHINGTON.

AFTERWORD

I, Liliʻuokalani, by the Grace of God and under the Constitution of the Hawaiian Kingdom, Queen, do hereby solemnly protest against any and all acts done against myself and the Constitutional Government of the Hawaiian Kingdom.

—The Queen

AN APOLOGY
Apologizing for a Lost Kingdom

TO ACKNOWLEDGE THE 100TH ANNIVERSARY of the January 17, 1893, overthrow of the Kingdom of Hawaii, and to offer an apology to Native Hawaiians on behalf of the United States for the overthrow of the Kingdom of Hawaii the United States Congress passed as a joint resolution Public Law 103-150.

No single act shaped modern Hawaii more than the end of the monarchy and the transformation of the islands from an agriculturally based economy to one that today is largely based on tourism. The bill, rarely reprinted except for here, as well as statements by leaders of the time offers important insights on why Hawaiians even today yean for the return of their kingdom.

Many Hawaiians consider this a host culture and those of us who came, and come from the so-called mainland guests. For anyone who wants to understand what Hawaii is all about, this is a must-read. The bill reads,

Prior to the arrival of the first Europeans in 1778, the Native Hawaiian people lived in a highly organized, self-sufficient, subsistent social system based on communal land ten-ure with a sophisticated language, culture, and religion.

Whereas, a unified monarchical government of the Hawaiian Islands was established in 1810 under Kamehameha I, the first King of Hawaii;

Whereas, from 1826 until 1893, the United States recognized the independence of the Kingdom of Hawaii, extended full and complete diplomatic recognition to the Hawaiian Government, and entered into treaties and conventions with the Hawaiian monarchs to govern commerce and navigation in 1826, 1842, 1875, and 1887;

Whereas, the Congregational Church (now known as the United Church of Christ), through its American Board of Commissioners for Foreign Missions, sponsored and sent more than 100 missionaries to the Kingdom of Hawaii between 1820 and 1850;

Whereas, on January 14, 1893, John L. Stevens (hereafter referred to in this Resolution as the "United States Minister"), the United States Minister assigned to the sovereign and independent Kingdom of Hawaii conspired with a small group of non-Hawaiian residents of the Kingdom of Hawaii, including citizens of the United States, to overthrow the indigenous and lawful Government of Hawaii;

Whereas, in pursuance of the conspiracy to overthrow the Government of Hawaii, the United States Minister and the naval representatives of the United States caused armed naval forces of the United States to invade the sovereign Hawaiian nation on January 16, 1893, and to position themselves near the Hawaiian Government buildings and the Iolani Palace to intimidate Queen Lili'uokalani and her Government;

Whereas, on the afternoon of January 17, 1893, a Committee of Safety that represented the American and European sugar planters, descendants of missionaries, and financiers deposed the Hawaiian monarchy and proclaimed the establishment of a Provisional Government;

Whereas, the United States Minister thereupon extended diplomatic recognition to the Provisional Government that was formed by the conspirators without the consent of the Native Hawaiian people or the lawful Government of Hawaii and in violation of treaties between the two nations and of international law;

Whereas, soon thereafter, when informed of the risk of bloodshed with resistance, Queen Liliʻuokalani issued the following statement yielding her authority to the United States Government rather than to the Provisional Government:

"I, Liliʻuokalani, by the Grace of God and under the Constitution of the Hawaiian Kingdom, Queen, do hereby solemnly protest against any and all acts done against myself and the Constitutional Government of the Hawaiian Kingdom by certain persons claiming to have established a Provisional Government of and for this Kingdom.

"That I yield to the superior force of the United States of America whose Minister Plenipotentiary, His Excellency John L. Stevens, has caused United States troops to be landed on Honolulu and declared that he would support the Provisional Government.

"Now to avoid any collision of armed forces, and perhaps the loss of life, I do this under protest and impelled by said force yield my authority until such time as the Government of the United States shall, upon facts being presented to it, undo the action of its representatives and reinstate me in the authority which I claim as the Constitutional Sovereign of the Hawaiian Islands." Done at Honolulu this 17th day of January, AD 1893.

Whereas, without the active support and intervention by the United States diplomatic and military representatives, the insurrection against the Government of Queen Lili'uokalani would have failed for lack of popular support and insufficient arms;

Whereas, on February 1, 1893, the United States Minister raised the American flag and proclaimed Hawaii to be a protectorate of the United States;

Whereas, a report on an investigation conducted by former Congressman James Blount into the events surrounding the insurrection and overthrow of January 17, 1893, concluded that the United States diplomatic and military representatives had abused their authority and were responsible for the change in government;

Whereas, as a result of this investigation, the United States Minister to Hawaii was recalled from his diplomatic post and the military commander of the United States armed forces stationed in Hawaii was disciplined and forced to resign his commission;

Whereas, in a message to Congress on December 18, 1893, President Grover Cleveland reported accurately on the illegal acts of the conspirators, described such acts as an "act of war, committed with the participation of a diplomatic representative of the United States and without authority of Congress," and acknowledged that by such acts the government of a peaceful and friendly people was overthrown;

Whereas, President Cleveland further concluded that a "substantial wrong has thus been done which a due regard for our national character as well as the rights of the injured people requires we should endeavor to repair" and called for the restoration of the Hawaiian monarchy;

Whereas, the Provisional Government protested President Cleveland's call for the restoration of the monarchy and continued to hold state power and pursue annexation to the United States;

Whereas, the Provisional Government successfully lobbied the Committee on Foreign Relations of the Senate (hereafter referred to in this Resolution as the "Committee") to conduct a new investigation into the events surrounding the overthrow of the monarchy; and annexation;

Whereas, the Committee and its chairman, Senator John Morgan, conducted hearings in Washington, DC, from December 27, 1893, through February 26, 1894, in which members of the Provisional Government justified and condoned the actions of the United States Minister and recommended of Hawaii;

Whereas, although the Provisional Government was able to obscure the role of the United States in the illegal overthrow of the Hawaiian monarchy, it was unable to rally the support from two-thirds of the Senate needed to ratify a treaty of annexation;

Whereas, on July 4, 1894, the Provisional Government declared itself to be the Republic of Hawaii;

Whereas, on January 24, 1895, while imprisoned in Iolani Palace, Queen Liliʻuokalani was forced by representatives of the Republic of Hawaii to officially abdicate her throne;

Whereas, in the 1896 United States Presidential election, William McKinley replaced Grover Cleveland;

Whereas, on July 7, 1898, as a consequence of the Spanish-American War, President McKinley signed the Newlands Joint Resolution that provided for the annexation of Hawaii;

Whereas, through the Newlands Resolution, the self-declared Republic of Hawaii ceded sovereignty over the Hawaiian Islands to the United States;

Whereas, the Republic of Hawaii also ceded 1,800,000 acres of crown, government and public lands of the Kingdom of Hawaii, without the consent of or compensation to the Native Hawaiian people of Hawaii or their sovereign government;

Whereas, the Congress, through the Newlands Resolution, ratified the cession, annexed Hawaii as part of the United States, and vested title to the lands in Hawaii to the United States;

Whereas, the Newlands Resolution also specified that treaties existing between Hawaii and foreign nations were to immediately cease and be replaced by United States treaties with such nations;

Whereas, the Newlands Resolution effected the transaction between the Republic of Hawaii and the United States Government;

Whereas, the indigenous Hawaiian people never directly relinquished their claims to their inherent sovereignty as a people or over their national lands to the United States, either through their monarchy or through a plebiscite or referendum;

Whereas, on April 30, 1900, President McKinley signed the Organic Act that provided a government for the territory of Hawaii and defined the political structure and powers of the newly established Territorial Government and its relationship to the United States;

Whereas, on August 21, 1959, Hawaii became the 50th State of the United States;

Whereas, the health and wellbeing of the Native Hawaiian people is intrinsically tied to their deep feelings and attachment to the land;

Whereas, the long-range economic and social changes in Hawaii over the nineteenth and early twentieth centuries have been devastating to the population and to the health and wellbeing of the Hawaiian people;

Whereas, the Native Hawaiian people are determined to preserve, develop and transmit to future generations their ancestral territory, and their cultural identity in accordance with their own spiritual and traditional beliefs, customs, practices, language, and social institutions;

Whereas, in order to promote racial harmony and cultural understanding, the Legislature of the State of Hawaii has determined that the year 1993, should serve Hawaii as a year of special reflection on the rights and dignities of the Native

Hawaiians in the Hawaiian and the American societies;

Whereas, the Eighteenth General Synod of the United Church of Christ in recognition of the denomination's historical complicity in the illegal overthrow of the Kingdom of Hawaii in 1893 directed the Office of the President of the United Church of Christ to offer a public apology to the Native Hawaiian people and to initiate the process of reconciliation between the United Church of Christ and the Native Hawaiians; and

Whereas, it is proper and timely for the Congress on the occasion of the impending 100th anniversary of the event, to acknowledge the historic significance of the illegal overthrow of the Kingdom of Hawaii, to express its deep regret to the Native Hawaiian people, and to support the reconciliation efforts of the State of Hawaii and the United Church of Christ with Native Hawaiians;

Now, therefore, be it Resolved by the Senate and House of Representatives of the United States of America in Congress assembled,

The Congress—

First, on the occasion of the 100th anniversary of the illegal overthrow of the Kingdom of Hawaii on January 17, 1893, acknowledges the historical significance of this event which resulted in the suppression of the inherent sovereignty of the Native Hawaiian people;

Second, recognizes and commends efforts of reconciliation initiated by the State of Hawaii and the United Church of Christ with Native Hawaiians;

Third, The Congress apologizes to Native Hawaiians on behalf of the people of the United States for the overthrow of the Kingdom of Hawaii on January 17, 1893, with the participation of agents and citizens of the United States, and the deprivation of the rights of Native Hawaiians to self-determination;

Fourth, expresses its commitment to acknowledge the ramifications of the overthrow of the Kingdom of Hawaii, in order to provide a proper foundation for reconciliation between the United States and the Native Hawaiian people; and

Fifth, urges the President of the United States to also acknowledge the ramifications of the overthrow of the Kingdom of Hawaii and to support reconciliation efforts between the United States and the Native Hawaiian people.

DICTIONARY OF HAWAIIAN WORDS

A
'aina - land
a hui hou - until we meet again
ali'i - chief

H
halau - hula school
hana ho encore - do it again
hanai - adopt
haole - foreigner, Caucasian
hapa, hapa haole - often refers to a Caucasian who also has Hawaiian ancestry, also often applied to songs
heiau - temple

I
ipu gourd - drum
iwi - bones, often refers to ancient bones

K
kahili - royal standard
kahu - reverend
kalo, taro - a plant used to make poi, often staple of Hawaiian diet
Kanaka Maioli - Native Hawaiian
kane - man
kanu - burials
kapa taro - plant
kapu - forbidden
keiki chilkumu - teacher
kohola - whale
kohole - naughty
kuleana - responsibility often referred to land or families
kumu hula - teacher of hula
kupuna - elder, wise person

L
limu - seaweed
luau - feast often with hula

M
mahalo - thank you
malama - take care of, often referring to the land
makai - toward the ocean
malihini - newcomer
malo loin cloth
mauka - toward the mountains
mana - personal power

N
na - adds plural to a word (there is no s in Hawaiian)
na ohana - family (plural]
niele - acquisitive

O
'ohana - family

P
ploku - long spear
pono - balance, proper, righteousness
puo - owl

T
talk story - a conversation
tutu - grandmother
U
uniki - hula class graduation

W
wai - water

PLACES

Hana - small town in east Maui home to many Hawaiians

Huelo - small town on the North Shore on the road to Hana

Kahului - largest town on Maui town in Central Maui begun as "the dream city"

Ka'anapali - Maui's largest resort community that opened in the early 1960;s and is the island's premier visitor destination

Kapalua - resort in northern part of West Maui

Kula - small town "up country" on the lower slopes of Haleakala Crater

Lahaina - historic town in West Maui base for missionaries and whaling

Lana'i - across channel from Lahaina, once known as the pineapple isle

Ma'alaea - small resort community with harbor midway between Lahaina and Wailuku

Makawao - cowboy town below Paia

Moloka'i - island across channel from Ka'anapali former site of leper colony

Olowalu - crossroads on the outskirts of Lahaina to the south

Paia - former hippy town on the North Shore site of wind surfing, once largest plantation town on Maui

Wailea - resort area on the coast far sould of Kahului

Wailuku - historic town, county seat

ABOUT THE AUTHOR

Norman G. Bezane, usually referred to as Norm, was finalist for the best columnist in Hawaii and the best independent journalist in 2015, has written more than 250 columns profiling Maui's Native Hawaiians, movers and shakers, colorful characters, artists, entrepreneurs, and preservationists.

In 2006, passionate about Maui like so many others and curious about Hawaiian culture and the lives of those who work and play here, the writer returned to his journalistic roots to write a column.

In Lahaina News, remarkable people of aloha are chronicled, those of Hawaiian heritage, those lucky enough to have been born here, and malihini. These are the people who shaped and are shaping modern Hawaii.

These tales dip into how Maui became Maui: how a captain became the first western visitor, a king united the islands, a queen lost a very progressive monarchy, missionaries brought a new religion, and entrepreneurs transformed the land.

Author's goal: to entertain, inform, and preserve the stories of movers and shakers of the last 50 years.

DEDICATION

Voices of Aloha: Beyond the Beach is dedicated to remarkable people, some of whom have passed, or individuals
and organizations that have shaped yesterday's and today's
Maui by preserving or enhancing the culture or improving
the visitor experience:

Charles Ka'upa, Ed Lindsey, kupuna ;Jim Luckey, preser-
vationist;Uwe Schulz, architect; Sammy Kadotani, old-tim-
er; Charles Maxwell, activist; Emma Farden Sharpe, Kumu
Hula.

The Lahaina Restoration Foundation, the Ritz-Carlton,
Kapalua, Mau Arts & Cultural Center, Old Lahaina Luau,
Trilogy Excursions, Lahaina Galleries.

ACKNOWLEGMENTS

The author is indebted to every one of these voices of Maui for the willingness to sit down for an interview and share their life stories and views of this dynamic culture.

Hawaiians Malihini Keahi Heath and David Kapaku have been particularly helpful in assuring that the text respects the culture and is accurate.

Most of the books in the Voices of Maui series have been produced and proofed solely by the author with sometimes disturbing results in the typography department.

Finally, but certainly not least in the tradition of every author, my wife, Sara, merits a salute. And let us not forget the little dog Kea Aloha, six years old, who once again co-operated by not eating the manuscript for breakfast and not knocking over the laptop. We leave it Kea Aloha to offer up for a final farewell.

VOICES OF ALOHA SERIES

Voices of Maui books are available online at
normbezane.com
and at some local stores on Maui.

FEEDBACK AND DIALOGUE

Readers are encouraged to write reviews for
Amazon or send comments to the author at
normmauiauthor@gmail.com

Blogs. Updates on Maui happenings can be found
on my blog,
normbezane.com or **joysofkaanapali.com**

IN MEMORY

Joan Bezane White, Carol Coe, Sr., Ed Lindsey,
Jim Luckey, Sammy Katotano, Uwe Schultz, Blackie
Gadarian, Queen Lili'uokalani, King Kamehameha
the Great, Queen Ka'ahamanu

ALOHA

Made in the USA
San Bernardino, CA
14 January 2018